ESSAYS ON AMERICAN FOREIGN POLICY

The Walter Prescott Webb Memorial Lectures: VIII

THE WALTER PRESCOTT WEBB MEMORIAL LECTURES

ESSAYS ON AMERICAN FOREIGN POLICY

BY

DAVID C. DeBOE

VAN MITCHELL SMITH

ELLIOTT WEST

NORMAN A. GRAEBNER

Preface by Llerena Friend

Introduction by Robert H. Ferrell

Edited by Margaret F. Morris and Sandra L. Myres

PUBLISHED FOR THE UNIVERSITY OF TEXAS AT ARLINGTON
BY THE UNIVERSITY OF TEXAS PRESS, AUSTIN AND LONDON

Thanks are expressed to the following for permission to quote:

General Services Administration, Franklin D. Roosevelt Library, Hyde Park,
New York, for the Roosevelt Papers.
Harper & Row Publishers, Inc., for *The Strategy of Peace*, by John F. Ken-
nedy, edited by Allan Nevins; and *The United States in World Affairs*, ed-
ited by Richard P. Stebbins.
Houghton Mifflin Company for *A Thousand Days*, by Arthur Schlesinger.
MacMillan Publishing Co., Inc., and Weidenfeld and Nicolson Ltd. for *The
Kennedy Legacy*, by Theodore C. Sorensen (Copyright © 1969 by Theodore
C. Sorensen).
Yale University Library, New Haven, Connecticut, for the Henry L. Stimson
Papers.

Library of Congress Cataloging in Publication Data
Main entry under title:

Essays on American foreign policy.

   (The Walter Prescott Webb memorial lectures, 8)
   Includes bibliographies.
   CONTENTS: DeBoe, D. Secretary Stimson and the Kellogg-Briand pact.—
Smith, V. M. Africa: the Kennedy years, 1961–1963. [etc.]
   1. United States—Foreign relations—20th
century—Addresses, essays, lectures. I. DeBoe,
David C., 1942–   II. Myres, Sandra L., ed.
III. Morris, Margaret F., 1938–   ed.
IV. Series
E744.E87   327.73   73-19500
ISBN 0-292-72009-2   ISSN 0083-713X

CONTENTS

PREFACE

The eighth annual Walter Prescott Webb Memorial Lectures were held at the University of Texas at Arlington on March 22, 1973. Following the format of previous years, members of the University of Texas at Arlington faculty presented the morning lectures: Professor David C. DeBoe spoke on Secretary Stimson and the Kellogg-Briand Pact; Professor Van Mitchell Smith discussed President Kennedy's African policy, 1961–1963; and Professor Elliott West presented an analysis of how the American press viewed the Soviet Union, 1941–1947. During the evening, the distinguished diplomatic historian, Professor Norman A. Graebner of the University of Virginia, delivered a lecture entitled "Japan: Unanswered Challenge, 1931–1941."

In past years it has been customary for the editors to write a preface to each volume, summarizing the papers and dedicating the essays to Walter Prescott Webb, the eminent historian and teacher whose memory is honored by the lecture series. This year, 1973, marked the tenth anniversary of Dr. Webb's tragic and untimely death. At the luncheon on March 22, honoring Webb's friends and former students, Dr. Llerena Friend, his longtime associate, delivered a delightful and eloquent tribute to this great scholar. The Webb Lecture Committee and the editors be-

lieve there could be no more fitting preface to this volume than
to present, in lieu of the editors' introduction, the text of Dr.
Friend's luncheon address.

Margaret F. Morris
Sandra L. Myres

This I Remember

A casual reference dropped by W. P. Webb in a history class in 1927 introduced me to *The Education of Henry Adams*. On page 353 of that book there is a profound statement: "Nothing is more tiresome than a superannuated pedagogue." With that thought in mind, I'll try to eliminate some of the purely personal, hoping instead to introduce some "Webbisms" that recall a warm and humane and very human person. To those who did not know Dr. Webb I apologize in advance for taking much for granted; to those who did know him I'll admit that I'm forced to omit the masculine approach of a Joe Frantz or a Bert Barksdale, and I may fail to choose the most vivid anecdotes and relate them well. But, each of us has his own set of memories.

George Wolfskill asked me to draw on personal recollections of the individual celebrated on this occasion at the University of Texas at Arlington, an institution in which he had great interest and one that all his former students honor for thus honoring him.

To be honest, I don't remember Dr. Webb before the fall of 1923, when the University of Texas at Austin opened its fall session, with me a senior and, for the second year, a grader in History 9. The year before, I had graded for Professor Duncalf in that class in modern European history. Now Webb had returned to the campus to handle the big section that met three times a week in the large lecture room in the Law Building. I know now that the year before Webb had been experiencing perdition as a graduate student in the University of Chicago. I was then ignorant of graduate work—by him or anyone else. I more or less graded the papers in History 9, usually the long omnibus question, and I also accompanied Webb over to the then Education Building to his class that had to do with the teaching of history. It was noncredit for me, but I did take some notes, and what good fortune that turned out to be. I had avoided education courses and had no practice teaching; yet the very next year I plunged into teaching five classes in history and civics in Vernon High School. From Webb I had at least heard the words "lesson plan" and something on the merits of out-lining.

In the spring of 1924, he and I were crossing from the Law Building to Old Main's "English Channel," where Webb of-ficed, carrying arms full of blue books. I dropped mine when Webb exclaimed: "Look, look at that man. He is the villain in *The Golden Cocoon*." With that remark the professor became a human being; he read novels—and novels about Austin at that.

After three years of teaching I returned to the University to work on the M.A. degree. I had a fellowship of $250.00 and had borrowed $500.00 to cover the year. During that graduate year I had my first Webb course for credit—and history for *me* became "High Adventure." Without knowing what a seminar was or ever having heard the term mentioned, I had one. In that senior course in American history, he asked the students to un-dertake special investigations and write a paper to be read to the class. I remember that mine entailed aspects of the Homestead Law—particularly the inadequate size of homestead units in the Arid West. By dint of wonderful serendipity (he introduced me to that term) I encountered a book with which Webb was not ac-

quainted. He rejoiced, and how I profited! I did not have to prepare a second paper for the spring semester. In June 1928, I got
a thesis signed and the degree conferred, but I had no money
left to get home. Webb created one of four jobs from which I
managed to accumulate enough to pay board and room for the
first term of summer school and have train fare home. I know
now that I'm not the only person for whom jobs somehow mi-
raculously appeared. Paul Crume relates a similar experience in
1936, a time when it was hard to see the next meal ahead. He
said that Dr. Webb could always find, tactfully, a bit of research
that needed to be done for pay. Thus, on *Divided We Stand*,
Crume had the job of counting all the drugstores in the United
States to see how many were chain owned. Crume says that Webb
made no use of his research in the book, but that it probably in-
fluenced him a lot on what to leave out. The job that Webb gave
to me was checking footnotes and bibliography for *The Great
Plains*. I doubt it was any benefit to him, but I learned the bibliography of the West. After the book was published, he wrote me:
"I'm holding the autographed copy of the book until you come
to Austin. Seriously, I expect to give you one but I'm somewhat
in the position of the Indian who was urged to become a Christian. I can't do it just yet."

By 1936, I was teaching history in Wichita Falls, including
the newly offered course in Texas history. That year I happened
to be president of the Wichita Falls City Teachers Association
with the responsibility for securing the speaker for the annual
banquet. *The Texas Rangers* was just out; I asked Webb to come
as speaker. He came, complete with the original Lonnie Reese
drawings to illustrate his talk. We had a dinner, a successful
meeting, and a puffed-up president until some older teacher—
feminine—opined in my presence that it was unfortunate to
have brought in such a poor speaker; she knew many who would
have been more eloquent. It gave me great joy, not long after, to

post on the faculty bulletin board the notice of Webb's appointment as Harkness Professor at the University of London. All
right, he was not an eloquent or forceful speaker; he was often
diffident, but he had the facts and he told them. With passing
years he developed considerable fluency on occasion, but his writ-
ings always surpassed his oral delivery. Anyhow, that night he
made the speech in Wichita Falls, he had already shoved *The
Texas Rangers* to the back of the stove and was absorbed in the
thesis of *Divided We Stand*, which he described to me during
the dinner. As Haley once wrote of him, "When he finished a
good piece of work, in good taste he laid it aside and apparently
forgot it." He searched for the proper name for *Divided We
Stand*, and I think perhaps it was well that he did not use that
suggested by his friend Trombly, "Oh South! Oh West!"

On one occasion my superintendent came back from Austin
and told me that Dr. Webb said I was to organize a chapter
of Junior Historians. And so I did, the charter for Group 6 being
granted at a mid-year meeting of the Texas State Historical Association here in Arlington. I used my Texas history class as nu-
cleus for the organization, persuaded them to interview old-tim-
ers for local stories, and bribed them with possibilities of a
spring trip to Austin to the annual meeting of TSHA. They
felt they were personally acquainted with all *Quarterly* contrib-
utors and the association staff personnel.

Among their other activities, my Junior Historians raised
money for a marker for the Texas Santa Fe Expedition, which
had crossed the Wichita River on August 4, 1841. The logical
speaker for the dinner on the occasion of unveiling the marker
would have been Bailey Carroll, from whose dissertation we
had secured the facts about the expedition, but Dr. Carroll was
teaching at El Paso and couldn't get off on August 4, 1941. Dr.
Webb came to Wichita Falls again—this time to a small but
select audience. His topic was "Paso por Aqui," one that he had

used in another context the spring before when he had been commencement speaker at the college in New Mexico not too far from the divide named for Eugene Manlove Rhodes, from whose book he had secured the title. I remember that after dinner that night we went out to visit with John Gould, newspaper man and Texas Ex, and John muttered to me as Dr. Webb sweetened his toddy, "How I hate to see good whiskey ruined with sugar."

In the summer of 1943 I did a stint of work on the list of suggested subjects for the projected *Handbook of Texas* and that summer assignment eventually turned into full time. The Webbs and the Carrolls took me out to Friday Mountain, where Dr. Webb pointed out each landmark and the reason for its name—and served wine made from the mustang grapes grown on the place. During part of the time when I was starting on the *Handbook* work, he was at Oxford, and after that wartime English experience he developed a taste for afternoon tea and wished that our campus had amenities that would allow for entertaining visiting faculty and other guests. With our campus bulging with returning GIs and classes meeting far into the night, it took a bit of doing for Betty Brooke Eakle and me to borrow china and lay in supplies for eastern visitors to have tea in Garrison Hall 105. The desks-and-mission-oak décor was a bit strange for a tea party. After the English experience he talked about English universities for the Philosophical Society of Texas and was scheduled to talk on the same subject to Phi Beta Kappa members. He forgot the engagement and had to be sent for, being located just before he was leaving for Friday Mountain.

For a semester or so, Webb conducted a night seminar on the writing of articles for the *Handbook*. On one occasion, his sometime puckishness with students was rewarded in kind. A student, in an article on the Czechs in Texas, commented on Czech food as an ethnic characteristic. That, Webb said, he would believe

when he had some of the food to sample. At the next meeting of
the seminar, the gal showed up with three huge boxes of kolaches. Those delectable prune goodies needed coffee; so I hurried
home to put on the coffee pot while the class adjourned there to
eat kolaches and listen to my collection of Texas records, including, as I recall, "I've Got a Gal Named Alice; Got a Wife
in Dallas." For the sake of the timing of the course, we couldn't
allow any more such diversions, however educational.

By the time that I was about to the end of my *Handbook* job,
and maybe to the end of my dissertation, there came a request
from Wichita Falls that I come home and write a history of the
community. I stopped by Room 102 to tell Dr. Webb about the
offer, and he said, "Why, you can't afford to upset your future
here." I stared blankly and asked, "What future?" He had always warned me that a woman's work on the Ph.D. was futile
from the standpoint of promotion or pay or any future in the
History Department. Then he told me of the Texas History
Center position and that I was slated to be librarian. For a year
I had to keep my mouth tightly closed before any moves were
made.

Webb had always been interested in Sam Houston, particularly after his Texas Ranger study showed Houston-Ranger interest
in Mexico, but he told me to have Dr. E. C. Barker supervise my
dissertation, which was to be a Houston biography. I did, much
to the later confusion of the graduate dean. Webb was present
for my final orals, when I proceeded to muff the first question.
He said that I finally retrieved it way out in left field. I was
greatly interested when I later read one of his letters to J. Frank
Dobie in which he said: "There has never been a time in my
life when I could pass the sort of examination given for the
Ph.D. I rarely sit in on one of these mediaeval ordeals that I
don't shudder for the candidate, and I am usually in his corner.
The standards of academic brutality ought to go up at least 10

per cent upon my retirement—in my sector of the institution."
I'm grateful that he was in my corner—and that I was there before his retirement.

After the degree business was over, we talked about a Houston biography under joint authorship, and he had a copy of the
dissertation to work on for revision. The next thing I knew, he
said that a joint authorship would not be fair, as the work would
be mine and the recognized name would be his. I didn't buy
that, but soon I heard, through the *Houston Post*, that the University Press would publish a Houston biography by Llerena
Friend. Having a friend on the Press publication board wasn't
bad either.

One Saturday morning, when I was holding the library by
myself, Webb called to say that he had to have a copy of *The
Texas Rangers* and that he was coming through the campus drive
in a taxi en route to a plane and would not have time to come up
to the library to get it. I couldn't leave; he couldn't come; so I
spotted the janitor below and dropped the book over the rail
outside the front window to the janitor, who raced to the taxi
with it and brought back the word: "He said you would probably never see the book again." I didn't. Dr. Webb was on his
way to the publishers for *The Story of the Texas Rangers*, the
edition for young people. The library could stand its loss, especially considering the fact that Webb and Dobie had initiated
the library's collection of authors' manuscripts—including the
scenario for the *Texas Rangers* movie. I really think Webb
wanted to get rid of that one anyway.

In 1961, in a coffee encounter at the Chuck Wagon, I told
the colonel of a projected trip to Europe, and he said he had a
commission for me. I was to find out if the London tubes still
featured his favorite advertisement, the one that ran

Under the spreading chestnut tree the village smithy stood;

The smith a mighty man was he; his Guinness done him good.
Would Guinness do the same for me? my Guinness, 'course it would.

You know that I promised to undertake the commission. The
morning before my departure, Webb called the library to say
that he had another chore. If I were going to Westminster Abbey, would I please hunt for a plaque in honor of William Booth,
even though Booth, he knew, was not buried in the Abbey. Of
course he was hunting for verification of the connection between
Booth and the words that to him signified Webb's obligation to
W. E. Hinds:

> Plant the seeds and fear not the birds
> For the harvest is not yours.

I found no plaque at Westminster. The verger there sent me on
to Bunhill Cemetery, where I could commune with John Bun-
yan and Susannah Wesley—but no Booth. By the time I located
the Booth grave site out in Putney, it was too late for me to
visit it; so I had to write that I had fouled out on Booth—
and on Guinness as well. The beer ad that year was three seals
balancing colored balls. But, in that same letter, I sent discreet
questions about his progress with a favorite person in San An-
tonio. Before I had left Austin, my library pages, all the wait-
resses at the Night Hawk, and many of the faculty were aware
that the professor was courting Mrs. Terrell Maverick. We were
all in his corner and rejoiced at his rejoicing. At the party for
the newlyweds given by Joe and Helen Frantz a few months
later, I was greeted by a beaming groom who said, "Llerena, I
think you know Mrs. Maverick!"

At one of the coffee sessions, I commented that a young friend
of mine, a medical student, was trying to decide whether or not
he should specialize in geriatrics, and Webb exclaimed, "Never

say that word; that is the ugliest word in the English language."
Knowing his aversion to the connotations attached to growing
old, his friends would but rejoice that his life to the last moment
was professionally and personally rewarding and exciting.

One time I went by his office to remind him that he had not
sent to the library some of his reprints of recent articles. He was
busy and growled, "Shut up, you know that eventually the library will get my literary remains." And so it was, and part of
my own retirement time has been enriched by working in these
literary remains to develop three subjects: the story of his "Talks
on Texas Books," his "Writing of *The Texas Rangers*," and
glimpses of Webb as revealed in his writing of book reviews.

The contents of the Webb papers are overwhelming because
there is so much that is fun to know: the Webbisms that one
longs to quote, the biographical details that are revealing. For
instance, his first published work was not that famous letter to
The Sunny South, which brought him to the attention of W. E.
Hinds, but an article in the *Breckenridge Democrat* of August
13, 1903, entitled "Back Home."

He taught country school on a second-grade certificate secured
by examination at the county seat before he entered the University. Of that experience he wrote: "I went out to improve my
ignorance on those who were a little less so. . . . I had to find a
school that had been overlooked, that for some reason could
not be taught, and then I had to find a way to teach it." His
salary was $42.50 a month. At the age of twenty-one he entered
the University on "individual approval," and Charlie Potts was
the one who let him in. Above all else he ached to write, but of
his English classes at the University of Texas he wrote, "By the
end of my English courses I was so word conscious, so comma
blind, and so sentence-structure minded that I could not write a
paragraph."

H. Y. Benedict, the only other arts and science major who up to that time had gone to the University from Stephens County, got Webb a job that paid $200.00 a year at the University Co-op. In his senior year, Webb wrote four articles for the *Brecken- ridge Democrat*, describing the University of 1915—and its in- fluence on students from his part of the world. He depicted Bene- dict as one of the most civilized and humane men that Texas had then produced. That civilized and humane dean wrote to Webb on September 23, 1916:

> My dear Webb—I thought when you were over to see me last that you looked rather flossy—"dressed up" we used to call it in ancient times, but I did not dream that so fell a purpose lurked in your pal- pitating bosom. I wondered why I didn't hear further from you—now I know—non compos mentis—with job. That you two have my very best wishes goes without saying, still, I'll put it down.
>
> Yours most sincerely,
> H. Y. Benedict

The other of the twosome was Jane Oliphant of Austin, whom Webb had met in one of his classes and to whom he was married in the fall of 1916, just before taking a teaching job in San An- tonio. Mrs. Jane Webb died in 1960.

And I must interpolate here that another collection of Webb material, some of it literary remains, but also a rich collection of personal correspondence with his mother and with Jane Oli- phant Webb, has just been made available in the presentation of the collection to the Texas State Archives by Mr. C. B. Smith. Users of that collection should remember another Webbism: "All my life I have loved a post office, and with good reason, because most good things have come to me through the mail."

In August 1957, Webb reviewed a book called *Buckskin and Blanket Days* and commented about the author, "I doubt that any man would write an autobiography if he were not an egotist." In the last book review that he ever wrote, however, he indicated the importance of some biographies and autobiographies. The book was Allan Bosworth's *New Country*, which was the same country that Webb had known between 1892 and 1910. He said of Bosworth's book:

I think the book is important because it records the end of Epoch I of our history, the end of the frontier. . . . It is important for a second reason: it records that period in which the change in the way of living was greater in one life time than it had been in any previous thousand years. The biographies and the autobiographies that are being written now are of more importance than the public or the literary critics realize, important because they are recording an elbow in history, a change of direction, the passing of one age and the introduction to another one which as yet has no name.

Two decades before, in his own unpublished autobiography, called "Story of a Texan" and written while he was at Oxford, Webb had recorded that his own life "displayed a phase of Texas and American life in the transition period between the open frontier into which I was born and the closed planned world into which I had been carried, not too willingly, by the passive process of living."

Passively he may have lived, but actively he left his influence —on his colleagues, his students, his institution, and American historiography and letters.

Llerena Friend

INTRODUCTION

The foreign relations of the United States changed enormously during the years covered by the following essays. At the beginning of the 1930's, the then secretary of state, Henry L. Stimson, was meditating over the seemingly grand question as to whether the American government should consult with other interested governments in event of a serious breach of the peace by an aggressor nation. Thirty years later, in the early 1960's, American concerns had spread even to the problems of Africa, where three dozen or so new nations were emerging out of the old European empires.

How slowly, falteringly, humanly (one might say) the country's leaders moved to meet the challenge of events. Consider the case of Stimson, a respected New York lawyer and dedicated public servant, as ably set out by David C. DeBoe. Stimson sensed with a feeling approaching clarity that the forces of disorder and immorality in the world were pushing for a Second World War. With premonition on his side, he nonetheless had to contend with a pacific-minded president and with the mass of his countrymen whose daily lives were being filled with problems of the Great Depression. In construing the Kellogg-Briand Pact of 1928 as implying consultation among its signatories in

event of the pact's breach, he was trying to hit upon some principle of policy that would be acceptable to President Herbert Hoover and the Amerian people. When the Hoover administration
went down to defeat at the polls in 1932, he did not hesitate to
approach the incoming Roosevelt administration, and the result
was a conference with the president-elect at Hyde Park, which
if not conclusive was fairly successful, at least to the point of
Roosevelt's announcing that he and Stimson were in agreement.
The events of subsequent years—the degeneration of peace on
the Continent because of Hitler's subversion of the Treaty of
Versailles, the increasing turmoil in the Pacific symbolized by
the militarization of the Japanese government—were often to
obscure the force of any ideas that, perhaps, lodged in Roosevelt's mind during the discussions with Stimson. The retired secretary of state, again busy with his law practice in New York,
could comfort himself that he had done his best with, as he and
McGeorge Bundy later put it, spears of straw and swords of ice.

Just why the Japanese government—so prosperous by the
1970's despite the havoc of the Second World War, despite the
loss of territories gained by the conquests beginning in 1931—
chose to attack the United States in 1941 must remain a challenge to the analytical ingenuity of historians. Norman A.
Graebner, in a carefully argued essay, shows how the American
government under President Roosevelt and Secretary of State
Cordell Hull proved inflexible toward Japanese imperial ambitions, and this inflexibility together with the increasing sense of
desperation among Japan's military leaders brought a result that,
while theoretically predictable, seemed at the outset of the decade 1931–1941 almost inconceivable between two nations that
for almost a century, since the opening of Japan by Commodore
Perry in 1853–1854, had managed to solve their problems by
peaceful means. Most historians today would agree with Graeb-

ner about the administration's inflexibility, though it is necessary to point out the peculiar result of the Japanese attack in December 1941: the attack propelled the United States into the
Second World War, and otherwise the country might have remained neutral for many more months, perhaps long enough to
permit Hitler a victory or a stalemate over Russia, and thereby
allow the Nazi regime to finish off all the *Untermenschen* of
Europe instead of, as it turned out, only seven or eight million of them.

Elliott West's essay considers the drastic changes in the image
of Russia evidenced in the American press in 1941–1947: how,
at the outset of the Second World War, when Russia had allied
with Germany in the destruction of Poland and a few months
later attacked Finland, Americans were almost consumed by hostility toward the USSR; of how, during the years 1941–1945,
when the Germans were fighting the Russians, the image of the
Soviet Union changed; and of how, after the war, when frictions
and then serious disagreements arose between Washington and
Moscow, another drastic shift occurred that was clearly evident
by the time of the Truman Doctrine in 1947. To recall these
changes in the Russian image is, one must say, exceedingly use-
ful. By the early 1970's a school of historical "revisionists," a
small group of historians and publicists, was contending that
American policies in 1945–1947 had produced the cold war in
its most glacial proportions. West's essay is based on a detailed
study of newspaper and magazine opinion for the period 1939–
1947; it takes the position that opinion during the war years had
shifted so dramatically, the education of the American public
and of its leaders had been in such fits and starts, that disillusion
after the war was almost ordained. There was, he relates, a near
inevitability (historians believe nothing in history is inevitable)
about the cold war; postwar problems probably were not caused

by the policies stressed by historical revisionists, so much as by
the sheer disappointment of unfulfilled dreams. As a disbeliever
in cold war revisionism, I could not agree more fully. And yet in
view of the historical passions of the early 1970's I sense that
West's essay, more than the others in this volume, will provoke
a considerable dissent.

The essay by Mitchell Smith focuses on policy toward Africa
during the Kennedy years, and rightly, since this long neglected
part of the world became important when, commencing in 1956,
the African states began to emerge, and when in 1960 the Congo
disturbances brought Africa to the attention of the world. The
Kennedy administration, with its stress not merely upon the ap-
pearance of youth but also the expertness of youth, sought to
bring the country's youthful, liberal-minded talent to bear upon
African problems, and for a brief interlude, before Camelot
came to its flashing end, a new American foreign policy seemed
to be developing. Kennedy could not solve all problems in his
thousand days of power, but the willingness of his administration
to move with the tide of hope that had engulfed black Africans
—a feeling that the richest nation of the world was in some
manner to help Africans: the effort to assist, to instruct, to up-
lift (if one may use a word from another era)—gave promise
of a new policy toward the less developed places of the world.
There was something attractive about policy toward Africa in
those years—the photographs of the shaving-cream heir, G.
Mennen (Soapy) Williams, assistant secretary of state for African affairs, listening to the complaints of everyday Africans, or
even the cartoon that showed Soapy in the midst of an assem-
blage that resembled Dr. Livingstone's era, with the caption
reading, "And I said to Soapy . . ." Vietnam of course over-
whelmed the vision.

In the cataclysm of World War and the anxieties of cold war

the world thus had changed. From Henry Stimson to Mennen Williams was as large a transition as any thirty years in all of world history, perhaps larger. American historians are seeking to record and analyze this change, and doing it with success, as the following essays so well demonstrate.

ROBERT H. FERRELL

ESSAYS ON AMERICAN FOREIGN POLICY

Secretary Stimson and the Kellogg-Briand Pact

DAVID C. DeBOE

WHEN HENRY LEWIS STIMSON died in 1950, one of the most remarkable careers in American history came to an end. Under seven administrations, spanning nearly half a century, he had served in high office. Under Theodore Roosevelt he was U.S. attorney for the southern district of New York. In Taft's cabinet he was secretary of war. He was a colonel in the army under Wilson. Coolidge sent him to Nicaragua as a special executive agent and later to the Philippines as governor general. He was Hoover's secretary of state. Under Franklin D. Roosevelt and Harry Truman he was again war secretary.

Yet Stimson's distinction lay not merely in the length of his service and the variety of public offices he held. He made and helped to make decisions that literally shook the entire world. Much has been written about his action-filled life. Both critics and admirers, however, have focused particularly on his role as secretary of war before and during the Second World War. As war secretary, Stimson helped to plan diplomatic moves and defenses in the Pacific area during the months preceding the Jap-

anese attack at Pearl Harbor. The phrase "how we should ma-
neuver Japan into the position of firing the first shot" was his.
The "war warning" to the army command in Hawaii—a message that was so interpreted as to leave American planes at the
mercy of the Japanese—was also his. Thus Stimson had much
to do with the entry of the United States into the Second World
War. From the beginning of the war he was chief presidential
adviser on atomic policy and played a key role in the decision
to drop the atomic bomb on Hiroshima and Nagasaki.[1]

A less studied aspect of Stimson's remarkable career was his
earlier attempt to change the direction of American foreign policy. While Hoover's secretary of state, he sought to turn America away from isolationism. By means of the Kellogg-Briand
Pact, he hoped to bring the United States into collective action
for the preservation of peace. In these efforts to force America
to assume its obligations as a world power, he encountered opposition from all sides—from President Hoover, from Congress, and especially from public opinion. Stimson's fight against
such odds is a fascinating study in frustration.

In 1917 the United States abandoned its traditional policy of
noninvolvement when it joined the Allies in waging war against
the Central Powers. During the remainder of the First World
War and at the Paris Peace Conference, Woodrow Wilson took
the lead in erecting permanent machinery for the preservation of
world peace. His League of Nations was designed as a system of
collective action that would prevent wars in the future. The president's hopes for a new order, however, were shattered when the
U.S. Senate refused to join his league.

Once the war was won, the American people preferred to return to isolationism. In reality, such a return was not possible.

[1] Richard Nelson Current, *Secretary Stimson: A Study in Statecraft*,
pp. 3–5.

As the world's leading industrial and economic power, the United States was forced to become involved in delicate economic and political questions. The destruction of Europe's economic power by the war left America no alternative but to take the leadership in reconstructing the international economic system in order to preserve its trade relationships. Moreover, Japanese expansion in the Pacific further dictated a retreat from isolationism. The growth of the Japanese navy contained the threat of aggression. Such moves would necessarily involve the United States through America's possession of the Philippines.

Despite the fact that isolationism was unworkable, the American people clung to the belief that noninvolvement best served the national interest. Yet, while wanting to remain aloof from the rest of the world, America also desired peace. This peace sentiment was naive and born of a romantic delusion as to how the United States could best serve mankind. Americans wanted peace, to be sure, but they were unwilling to assume any obligations necessary to enforce an international system to guarantee peace. This fact was vividly revealed in the movement that culminated in the signing of the Kellogg-Briand Pact in 1928.

The idea of outlawing war originated with the American intellectual community in the early 1920's. The proposal entered the diplomatic realm when it was taken up by French Foreign Minister Aristide Briand. Perceiving an opportunity to draw the United States and France together in a sympathetic alliance, Briand proposed in 1927 that the United States and France sign a treaty outlawing war. Aware of Paris's motives, Secretary of State Frank B. Kellogg at first planned to ignore Briand's appeal. When public opinion demanded acceptance, however, the administration had to capitulate. Unwilling to sign a bilateral pact with France, which Coolidge and Kellogg regarded as a negative military alliance, they countered by suggesting that

France and the United States invite other powers to join them
in a treaty renouncing war as an instrument of national policy.[2]

The result was the Kellogg-Briand Pact signed in Paris in
August 1928. The treaty provided that the contracting powers
"condemn recourse to war for the solution of international controversies, and renounce it as an instrument of national policy,"
and that "the settlement or solution of all disputes . . . shall never be sought except by pacific means."[3] The treaty was signed
eventually by sixty-two nations. The U.S. Senate ratified it by the
overwhelming vote of eighty-one to one. The Senate, as well as
the man on the street, accepted the treaty at face value.

The treaty established no enforcement machinery and would
be only as effective as the signatories made it. But the Kellogg-
Briand Pact was not meaningless. For one thing, by outlawing
aggressive war it changed international law. For another, it
brought the United States into the peace structure. While Washington assumed no legal obligations under the pact, the American government did assume moral obligations to cooperate with
the signatories in the event that an aggressor violated it. Thus
the Kellogg-Briand Pact was not, as some historians have asserted, a mere "empty gesture" or an "international kiss."[4] For, as
Briand wisely observed at the time, the pact was a "beginning,
not an end."[5]

At least one man saw this pact as more than a meaningless
gesture. Henry L. Stimson, who became President Hoover's secretary of state in 1929, was aware of the pact's true potential.

[2] A comprehensive study of the negotiations of the Kellogg-Briand
Pact is Robert H. Ferrell, *Peace in Their Time: The Origins of the Kellogg-Briand Pact.*

[3] The full text of the Kellogg-Briand Treaty can be found in *Foreign
Relations of the United States: Diplomatic Papers, 1928*, I, 153–157.

[4] Current, *Secretary Stimson*, p. 46.

[5] Quoted in Arthur S. Link, *American Epoch: A History of the United
States Since the 1890's*, p. 354.

For him the Kellogg-Briand Pact was a tool by which the United States could accept its responsibilities as a world power in collaboration with other nations. Stimson entered the State Department in 1929 when the world was at peace, although during his term of office the peace structure erected at Versailles began to collapse. Aware that America's isolationist policies were inadequate, Stimson groped for a program that would bring the United States into collective security. The Kellogg-Briand Pact became his means to that end.

Although Stimson's ideas about the pact were not fully formulated until the Geneva Disarmament Conference, which met from 1932 to 1934, the treaty played an important role in the administration's handling of two earlier international disputes involving the Chinese province of Manchuria. The first minor incident occurred when Russian and Chinese troops clashed in Manchuria in 1929. During the conflict Stimson invoked the pact when he reminded Russia and China of their obligations as signatories of the treaty.[6]

A far more serious crisis occurred when Japan moved to consolidate her position in Manchuria in the fall of 1931. This conflict, which did not end until Japan established the puppet state of Manchukuo, was the first serious challenge to the international peace structure erected after the First World War. This time Stimson went much further. On repeated occasions he cited the pact in protesting Japanese aggressions. More important was his attempt to use the pact to bring the United States into collective security.

When the invasion began, China appealed to the League of Nations. The league had to consider what action—if any—should be taken in behalf of China. Japan, by going to war, had

[6] An account of the crisis is to be found in Robert H. Ferrell, *American Diplomacy in the Great Depression: Hoover-Stimson Foreign Policy, 1929–1933*, pp. 45–67.

also violated the Kellogg Treaty. On Stimson's urging, Hoover agreed to let an American representative sit with the League Council for the purpose of discussing the pact.[7] Such action constituted an abrupt departure from past policy. Until then Washington had shunned such cooperation with the league. For the first time the United States joined with others to discuss collective action to preserve peace. This was a first and long step away from isolationism. For the American public, such a step was permissible because of the grave situation caused by Japan's aggression. However, this decision did not change the general trend of popular thinking. American cooperation with the league otherwise suggested involvement in the political affairs of Europe and was unacceptable.

A second departure from isolationism, U.S. participation in the disarmament conference that convened at Geneva in 1932, was concealed under the slogan "peace through disarmament." On February 2, 1932, representatives from the United States and fifty-eight other nations met in Geneva for the first session of the League of Nations' World Disarmament Conference. This conference, until its adjournment in June 1934, occupied the center stage of international affairs. Many of the momentous events that took place in Europe from 1932 to 1934—the rise of national socialism to power in Germany, the shift in the British position from sympathy for Germany to alignment with France, the withdrawal of Germany from the League of Nations—are clearly mirrored in the proceedings at Geneva.

In the United States, advocacy of American cooperation with the League of Nations, suggesting as it did involvement in the

[7] Accounts of the second Manchurian crisis in American foreign relations may be found in Armin Rappaport, *Henry L. Stimson and Japan, 1931–1933*; and in Sara R. Smith, *The Manchurian Crisis, 1931–1932: A Tragedy in International Relations*. Stimson's personal account is contained in Henry L. Stimson, *The Far Eastern Crisis: Recollections and Observations*.

political affairs of Europe, was generally unpopular. But "peace through disarmament" was a slogan that enjoyed wide popularity and appealed to the illusion of a peaceful but noninvolved co-existence. Hence, this participation in the league's disarmament efforts was politically respectable to Republicans and Democrats alike. The American people did not understand that any discussion of world disarmament necessitated involvement with delicate European political questions. The screen of disarmament effectively concealed efforts to resolve these major questions of power politics and thus allowed American participation in the league's discussions.

As soon as the conference opened, it became apparent that disarmament was no simple matter. Relatively minor details turned into touchy political questions. The problem that weighed most heavily on the delegates was Article 5 of the Treaty of Versailles. Article 5 had obligated Germany at the time of her defeat to reduce her army, navy, and air forces to specified limits "in order to render possible the initiation of a general limitation of the armaments of all nations." During two years of negotiations, the delegates attempted to resolve the controversy between France and Germany as to the meaning of this article.

The Germans contended that their forced disarmament under Article 5 of the *Diktat* of Versailles was coupled with the understanding that the other major powers would also disarm. The French retorted that, although the German contention was true, this disarmament could proceed only within a "framework of security for all nations." France, it was argued, had accepted the obligations of the peace settlement with reservations that had not been fulfilled: the participation of the United States in the League of Nations and British and American guarantees of the French frontier.[8] The dispute ran in monotonously repetitive

[8] Two treaties, one between France and Great Britain, the other between France and the United States, signed June 28, 1919, guaranteed as-

circles that inevitably seemed to return to the failure of the United States to accept involvement.

Initially, Washington perceived its role at the conference as one of helping others find solutions to problems that did not directly concern the United States. By the summer of 1932, America's position had changed. It was then that Stimson attempted to clarify America's new policy of cooperation with the league, using, once again, the Kellogg-Briand Pact to solve the crucial deadlock at the conference: Germany's demand for equality in armaments and France's demand for security.

The main object of French foreign policy in 1932, as it had been in 1919 and in the years thereafter, was the organization of a system of security that would remove from French minds the haunting fear of another German invasion. With the knowledge that Germany was potentially far stronger than France, Paris had sought to reinforce her position by ties with other members of the international community: by guarantees from countries like Great Britain and the United States, who were less concerned with their own security; by pressure exerted through the peace settlement to strip Germany of her capacity for aggression; and by treaties with the new states of Eastern Europe, who also feared a German attack. Although disarmament ran counter to the general trend of French foreign policy, Paris was willing to consider it as long as any reduction of arms was accompanied by a proportionate strengthening of the peace structure.[9]

---

sistance to France in the event of "unprovoked aggression" against her by Germany. The U.S. Senate refused to ratify the treaty involving the United States, and, British acceptance having been made contingent upon such ratification, both treaties became void.

[9] For a good discussion of French foreign policy between the two world wars, see Elizabeth R. Cameron, *Prologue to Appeasement: A Study in French Foreign Policy*; W. M. Jordan, *Great Britain, France, and the German Problem, 1918–1939*; and Arnold Wolfers, *Britain and*

If the United States was to make any contribution toward breaking the impasse at the conference, it had to find some means of enhancing France's feeling of security. A military alliance or league membership was out of the question, but the Kellogg-Briand Pact might provide an acceptable compromise. Ever since the conclusion of that pact, suggestions had been made that the United States might recognize an obligation to consult with other signatories in the event of a breach or threatened breach of the pact.[10] France obviously believed such a commitment to be of some value. At the London Naval Conference in 1930 and during Premier Pierre Laval's trip to Washington in the fall of 1931, the French had sought such a pledge. The Hoover administration, however, fearing an "isolationist uproar," had refused these French suggestions as being "politically impossible."[11]

Despite Hoover's initial coolness toward any commitment for consultation, Stimson became convinced that the United States should recognize the Kellogg-Briand Pact as an obligation to consult. During the spring of 1932, Stimson's thoughts were often centered on the consultation question. A trip to European capitals in April convinced him that an American pledge to consult would help France meet the German claims for equality of status. While returning home, he drafted the substance of a

---

France between Two Wars: Conflicting Strategies of Peace since Versailles.

[10] The exact meaning of "consultation" was the subject of disagreement, but at the least it meant "talking things over," either through conventional diplomatic channels or in a special conference called for that purpose. At the most, it might imply an obligation to join in whatever concerted action was agreed upon after the powers had designated the "aggressor."

[11] An account of the French attempt to get a pledge from the United States may be found in Ferrell, *American Diplomacy in the Great Depression*, pp. 94–105; the negotiations during the Laval visit are discussed in ibid., pp. 198–204.

statement, "as a result of cogitations of what I have seen during the trip," on possible American contributions toward the future of the Kellogg-Briand Pact.[12]

Once back in Washington, the secretary outlined his plans to Hoover and Senator William E. Borah, chairman of the Senate Committee on Foreign Relations. On May 16 he told the president that a statement of our obligations under the pact would do more toward "clearing up" our relations with the League of Nations and helping the disarmament conference than almost anything else the United States could do.[13] Although Stimson thought Hoover favored the proposition, he was discouraged when the president expressed his fears that such a statement might have disastrous effects on the up-coming presidential campaign.[14] On June 5 the secretary talked with Borah about his scheme. The senator seemed interested after Stimson assured him that any decision to consult on a specific controversy would be left in American hands.[15]

After the Republican[16] and Democratic[17] parties had drawn

[12] Stimson diary, entries for May 8 to May 14, 1932 (at sea), vol. 21, Henry L. Stimson Papers, Yale University Library. Unfortunately neither the State Department nor Stimson's personal records contain the speech he prepared.

[13] Stimson diary, entry for May 16, 1932, Stimson Papers, vol. 22.

[14] Stimson diary, entry for May 20, 1932, Stimson Papers, vol. 22.

[15] Stimson diary, entry for June 5, 1932, Stimson Papers, vol. 22.

[16] The Republican platform stated, "We favor enactment by Congress of a measure that will authorize our Government to call or participate in an international conference in case of any threat or nonfulfillment of Article II of the Treaty of Paris, Kellogg-Briand Pact." For a discussion of the fight to get this into the Republican platform, see Russell Morgan Cooper, *American Consultation in World Affairs: For the Preservation of Peace*, pp. 56–58.

[17] The plank in the Democratic platform adopted on July 2, 1932, stated, "We advocate a firm foreign policy . . . the Pact of Paris abolishing war as an instrument of national policy to be made effective by provisions for consultation and conference in case of threatened viola-

up platform planks favoring consultation in the event of a violation of the Kellogg Pact, Stimson again met with Hoover on this question. Undoubtedly the secretary thought these provisions would lessen the president's anxiety over political complications. He now outlined plans for a speech on American obligations under the Kellogg Pact. But the president was still reluctant. While agreeing with Stimson on the need for clarifying Washington's position on consultation, Hoover "shied" away from making a statement on the subject during the campaign unless the other candidate would do the same.[18]

Stimson was not to be put off so easily. By July 14 he had made up his mind to go ahead at all costs. He wrote in his diary that he planned to write the speech out, present it to the president, and "tell him I am going to make it unless he forbids me."[19] For the next ten days he spent a part of each day working on what he now termed his "magnum opus." After study, he became convinced that this speech not only would prove beneficial to the disarmament conference, but also could be valuable in case of renewed Japanese aggression. He noted in his diary of July 20:

During the morning I was developing some more of my plans for the future, particularly with regard to the Far East. The Japanese are still pushing on with their imperialist plan. It is evident that we are going to be up against the issue this fall. I am trying to think out ahead what to do. . . . This speech that I am at work on is really for the purpose of laying the foundation stone for the whole policy by giving my views of the Kellogg Pact and the importance of the concerted action of the nations under it.[20]

tions of treaties" (Cooper, *American Consultation in World Affairs*, pp. 58–59).

[18] Stimson diary, entry for June 29, 1932, Stimson Papers, vol. 23.
[19] Stimson diary, entry for July 14, 1932, Stimson Papers, vol. 23.
[20] Stimson diary, entry for July 20, 1932, Stimson Papers, vol. 23.

On July 25, Stimson took the completed speech to the president for his approval.[21] Hoover's reaction was again proof that the presidential campaign was uppermost in his mind. "This has been a black day," was the way Stimson began the record of his confrontation with Hoover. He went on to say that the president was dismayed for fear that William Randolph Hearst would use any allusion to the League of Nations to attack him. Stimson confided to his diary, "He is simply bringing down the record of his Administration in this campaign to the pattern of what Hearst is going to say about it. That is what made me sad."[22]

In the discussion that followed, the secretary of state went over his whole strategy in the disarmament conference and in the Far East, pointing out that his speech was the foundation stone for success in both instances. He then showed Hoover that there were two sides to the speech. First, he hoped to defend the Kellogg Pact against the attack that had been made upon it in the United States by the intelligentsia. Perhaps because the intelligentsia was "not very important so far as votes are concerned," Hoover had no objections to this section of the speech. It was the second theme that caused a confrontation. Hoover ob-

---

[21] The State Department, with the exception of Eugene A. Regnier, Stimson's military adviser, thought the proposed speech was a brilliant move. Stimson explained Regnier's views thus: "Regnier is the one person who is dissatisfied with my speech, but it comes from the fact that he is thinking of it in connection with an entirely different purpose. My speech is intended to support the Kellogg Pact as the fulcrum upon which eventually we will have our issue with Japan. The speech is intended to rally the European countries around that Pact, so that when the issue with Japan comes up, they will support us intelligently on this central element. Regnier is looking at it on the other hand as a journalistic effort to arouse sentiment in this country against Japan. This is not at all what I am looking for now" (Stimson diary, entry for July 25, 1932, Stimson Papers, vol. 23).

[22] Stimson diary, entry for July 27, 1932, Stimson Papers, vol. 23.

jected to Stimson's contention that Washington's consultation under the Kellogg-Briand Pact was the only way to prevent a clash with the League of Nations. In the argument that followed, Stimson felt that he had been less than entirely successful in convincing the president of the importance of a pledge to consult under the pact. Hoover's main concern was still public opinion. Stimson made the revealing comment in his diary that if Hoover was going to run his campaign according to what Hearst said, then "I must keep out of it."[23]

On July 28, Stimson spent the day on the "discouraging" task of rewriting those sections of the speech to which the president objected. Although he had to tone down his stand that the United States had a commitment to consult in the event of aggression, he did obtain Hoover's assent to a statement pointing out "the inevitable fact that consultation will follow the proper development of the Kellogg Treaty."[24] Even though the speech was not all that Stimson had hoped for, his labors were finished at last.

On August 8, Stimson delivered his address entitled "The Pact of Paris: Three Years of Development" before the Council on Foreign Relations in New York.[25] In it he declared. "War between nations was renounced by the signatories of the Briand-Kellogg Treaty. This means it has become illegal throughout practically the entire world. . . . Hereafter when two nations engage in armed conflict either or both of them must be wrong-doers—violators of this general treaty law. We no longer draw

[23] Ibid.

[24] Stimson diary, entry for July 28, 1932, Stimson Papers, vol. 23.

[25] On July 23, before Stimson had laid his final plans before the president, the secretary telephoned Walter Lippmann and asked the columnist if the Council on Foreign Relations wanted to hear a speech by the secretary. Lippmann checked with the members of the council and August 8 was finally decided upon (Stimson diary, entry for July 23, 1932, Stimson Papers, vol. 23).

a circle about them and treat them with the punctilios of the duelist's code. Instead we denounce them as lawbreakers." After noting that the pact rested upon the sanction of world public opinion and reviewing the actions taken to invoke it in the Far East, he added: "Another consequence which follows this development of the Briand-Kellogg Treaty . . . is that consultation between the signatories of the Pact when faced with the threat of its violation becomes inevitable."[26]

The reaction to Stimson's speech was not as bad as Hoover feared it might be, and three days after the address the president reinforced the "doctrine" of his secretary.[27] In his speech accepting the renomination to the presidency he asserted, "We shall, under the spirit of the pact, consult with other nations in times of emergency to promote world peace."[28] That the new "doctrine" had indeed become an integral factor in U.S. foreign policy was again emphasized by Stimson in a speech in Pittsburgh on October 26. He said, "Whenever a breach of the treaty is threatened by approaching hostilities, it implies a duty of consultation among other parties in order that public opinion may be mobilized against the impending disaster of war."[29]

This recognition of an obligation to consult was vitally important. Without it Europe could not be sure of the attitude of the United States. With it Europe could go forward with discussions of security, sanctions, and disarmament, confident that in an emergency Washington would at least consult and make her attitude known. Europeans were quick to express just such views.

---

[26] "The Pact of Paris: Three Years of Development," *Foreign Relations of the United States: Diplomatic Papers, 1932,* I, 575–583.

[27] For the press reaction to Stimson's speech, see the *Literary Digest,* August 20, 1932, p. 6.

[28] *New York Times,* August 12, 1932, p. 4.

[29] Henry L. Stimson, *The Work of the United States Government in the Promotion of Peace during the Past Three Years,* p. 11.

The London *Times*, for example, expressed the prevailing British sentiment when it said:

> Mr. Stimson's pronouncement yesterday on the implications of the Briand-Kellogg Pact marks a real step in advance in the organization of peace. It materially improves the prospects of the Disarmament Conference. The reluctance of some Powers to accept any effective measure of disarmament was based on a sincere belief that it would be unsafe to do so without a better guarantee of security from unaggressive nations than could be given by any formal paper guarantee. . . . His main point, the point upon which the world will seize, is that the Pact . . . necessarily carries with it the implication of consultation.
>
> There can be no doubt that, given this interpretation, the Briand-Kellogg Pact can be made, as Mr. Stimson says, "an effective reality" protecting the peace of the world.[30]

French Premier Edouard Herriot openly showed his gratification, voicing his approval through several newspapermen. The premier noted that it was very valuable for France to know that "in the opinion of American statesmen the pact already involved in itself the necessity for those consultations."[31]

Stimson's August 8 address was a high point in America's efforts to cooperate in a collective security system. Shortly thereafter, the new administration of Franklin D. Roosevelt, using the Stimson program, reinforced this commitment to collective action. Problems arose, however, when first France[32] and then Britain made it clear they would not be satisfied with a simple pledge to consult. In March 1933 the British government presented a program to the Geneva conference seeking a written pledge that the United States would agree to consult with other nations in the event of a breach of the Kellogg Treaty. In addi-

[30] "America and World Peace," *The Times*, August 9, 1932, p. 11.
[31] *New York Times*, August 12, 1932, p. 3.
[32] The French proposal is found in Wilson to Stimson, November 15, 1932, telegram, *Foreign Relations, 1932*, I, 380–386.

tion, London proposed that, if the United States agreed that a violation of the pact had occurred, the United States should refuse to supply any aggressor with arms and would refuse to protect its own citizens engaged in trade with the aggressor.[33] In essence, Britain sought to have the United States give up its traditional rights as a neutral. If approved, the London proposal would go far toward ending the isolationism of the United States.

Before committing itself to the British, the new administration sought Stimson's advice. The former secretary of state expressed approval of the plan, remarking that the steps advocated "followed directly the course which I had been striving to reach by executive evolution." The only doubt that Stimson raised concerned the method of presentation. In Stimson's mind, an executive declaration would be less likely than a formal treaty to create political troubles in the Senate.[34]

Heeding Stimson's advice, Roosevelt had Norman Davis, the head of the American delegation at the disarmament conference, spell out the new American position. On May 22, 1933, Davis declared the United States ready to reduce arms and to contribute to the organization of peace. Specifically, Davis said that, if the disarmament conference was a success, Washington was "willing to consult the other states in case of a threat to peace with a view of averting conflict." Furthermore, if the United States agreed with the other Kellogg-Briand Pact signatories that a nation was guilty of violating the peace, the United States would not hinder any collective efforts taken.[35]

American policy had become one of open cooperation with

[33] The full text of the British plan is found in *Foreign Relations of the United States: Diplomatic Papers, 1933*, I, 43–54.

[34] Stimson diary, entry for April 19, 1933, Stimson Papers, vol. 26.

[35] For Davis's speech, see Davis to Hull, May 19, 1933, telegram, *Foreign Relations, 1933*, I, 154–158.

other nations in collective security. Even though the declaration was hedged about with conditions and safeguards, the new policy was a significant step. The United States had agreed to discuss violations of the peace with other nations, and had agreed, if not to move against the aggressor, at least not to insist on traditional rights that would interfere with the efforts of others to restore peace. Henry L. Stimson's goal of making the Kellogg-Briand Pact a real influence had seemingly been attained under a new administration.

But the forces of isolationism in the U.S. Senate had not yet been heard. Their actions in the next few weeks were to undercut completely the new position on collective security. Since January of 1933 the Congress had been considering a series of resolutions to limit or forbid the shipment of arms and munitions when such shipment might promote or encourage war. As originally proposed, the president would have discretion to forbid the sale of arms to either one side or both sides in a conflict. Stimson hoped that such legislation would further bring the United States into collective security by enabling the president to cooperate with other signatories of the Kellogg Pact in isolating an aggressor nation.[36] Stimson even contemplated participation in league sanctions. He told the House Foreign Affairs Committee on February 9, 1933, that, if the league should designate an aggressor, "the participation of the United States in a general arms embargo would be not merely practical and sound, but practically necessary to preserve our national dignity and standing as a peaceful nation."[37] Thus, as Stimson conceived

[36] That foreign nations also saw the benefits of such legislation was clear from a conversation Stimson had with the French ambassador. The ambassador told the secretary that it was "exactly in line with what the French Government had long urged" (memorandum by the undersecretary of state, February 2, 1933, ibid., I, 359–360).

[37] Castle to Wilson, February 13, 1933, telegram, ibid., I, 361–362.

it, the arms-embargo legislation was an additional tool by which
the United States could cooperate with other nations.

The proposed legislation had not yet been passed when
Roosevelt became president. Thanks to Stimson, it quickly
gained the support of the new administration.[38] Roosevelt and
Cordell Hull, the new secretary of state, like Stimson, wanted
discretionary power in applying an arms embargo. In April the
House passed the measure, but it was held up in the Senate
Foreign Relations Committee. On May 17, Joseph Green of
the Western European division of the State Department, in re-
laying Hull's views to the committee, conceded that the administration might, under the proposed legislation, conceivably
levy an embargo against a violator of the Kellogg Pact.[39] Thereupon Senator Hiram Johnson introduced an amendment making
any arms embargo an impartial one to be applied to aggressor
and victim alike.

This amendment was, of course, completely contrary to the
policy that the administration had been following in Geneva and
urging upon Congress. It would make it impossible for Washington to cooperate with other countries against an aggressor.
It served notice to the world that the United States viewed ag-
gressors and victims with impartiality and indifference. Hull and
Roosevelt, soon after the amended resolution was introduced
into the Senate, made it known that they were opposed to the
amendment.[40] In the subsequent months, the administration suc-

---

[38] Robert A. Divine, *The Illusion of Neutrality*, p. 43.

[39] Cordell Hull, *The Memoirs of Cordell Hull*, I, 229; Divine, *The Illusion of Neutrality*, p. 53.

[40] Strangely enough, Roosevelt, without consulting Hull, told Key
Pittman, chairman of the Senate Committee on Foreign Relations, that
he would support the amended resolution. Once Hull explained to the
president, however, that the amended resolution was in conflict with
Davis's May twenty-second pledge, the president agreed to exert pressure
to kill the bill (Hull, *Memoirs*, I, 229–230).

cessfully prevented passage of the impartial arms-embargo resolution.

Even though the amended resolution died, these congressional deliberations had a profound effect on the disarmament conference and on the new administration. Quite naturally, Britain and France, which had had such hopes for U.S. cooperation, were disappointed. They now began to question whether the American people would follow their president in any move away from isolationism.[41] Perhaps even more significant was the effect that the deliberations had on Roosevelt. Using the Stimson plan, the new president had sought to bring the United States into a system of collective security. Now, like Hoover, he questioned the political wisdom of such action. In the months that followed, the administration began to retreat from its former position. No longer was it willing to assume obligations to preserve peace.

Just how far the State Department had retreated from the Stimson position became apparent during the Italo-Ethiopian Crisis of 1935. Whereas Stimson had used the Kellogg-Briand Pact to bring the United States into the league discussions during the Manchurian Crisis of 1931, the Roosevelt administration refused any cooperation with either the league or the Kellogg-Briand Pact signatories when Italy invaded Ethiopia.[42] Thus ended Stimson's plans for the United States and the Kellogg-Briand Pact.

[41] This view was made clear to the British ambassador in Paris when the French government informed him that it viewed the amended legislation as a "portent" of the difficulties Roosevelt would have in steering America from her isolationist course (Tyrrell [British Ambassador in Paris] to Simon [British Foreign Minister], June 7, 1933, telegram, *Documents on British Foreign Policy, 1919–1939*, ed. E. Llewellyn Woodward and Rohan Butler, Second Series, V, 330–334).

[42] The most complete account of the American role in the Italo-Ethiopian Crisis is Brice Harris, *The United States and the Italo-Ethiopian Crisis*.

Forgotten by the world and the United States during the late 1930's, the Kellogg-Briand Pact was resurrected in 1946 to legalize the Nuremberg and Tokyo war crimes trials. This idealistic document was used for less than idealistic purposes, as it was charged that Germany and Japan had violated their agreement not to resort to war. It was indeed ironic that the United States now claimed for purposes of retribution a document that Henry Lewis Stimson had asked them to claim for purposes of peace.

World War II changed the direction of U.S. foreign policy. Now the man on the street accepted our obligation to enforce peace—an acceptance that stood unchallenged through Korea, Lebanon, Cuba, the Dominican Republic, and the initial involvement in Vietnam. We are perhaps witnessing a new shift in direction. The question is how far the pendulum will swing.

BIBLIOGRAPHY

Atwater, Elton. *American Regulation of Arms Exports*. Washington, D.C.: Carnegie Endowment for International Peace, 1941.

Cameron, Elizabeth R. *Prologue to Appeasement: A Study in French Foreign Policy*. Washington, D.C.: American Council on Public Affairs, 1942.

Cooper, Russell Morgan. *American Consultation in World Affairs: For the Preservation of Peace*. New York: Macmillan Company, 1934.

Current, Richard N. "Consequences of the Kellogg Pact." In *Issues and Conflicts*, edited by George L. Anderson. Lawrence: University of Kansas Press, 1959.

————. *Secretary Stimson: A Study in Statecraft*. New Brunswick: Rutgers University Press, 1954.

DeBoe, David C. "American Policy at the Geneva Disarmament Conference, 1932–1934." Ph.D. dissertation, Tulane University, 1969.

Divine, Robert A. "F D R and Collective Security, 1933." *Mississippi Valley Historical Review* 58 (June 1961): 42–59.

————. *The Illusion of Neutrality*. Chicago: University of Chicago Press, 1957.

Ferrell, Robert H. *American Diplomacy in the Great Depression: Hoover-Stimson Foreign Policy, 1929–1933*. New Haven: Yale University Press, 1957.

————. *Peace in Their Time: The Origins of the Kellogg-Briand Pact*. New Haven: Yale University Press, 1952.

Fleming, Denna Frank. *The United States and World Organization, 1920–1933*. New York: Columbia University Press, 1938.

France, Ministère Des Affaires Étrangères. *Documents Diplomatiques Français, 1932–1939*. 1st series. 4 vols. to date. Paris: Imprimerie Nationale, 1964–.

Great Britain, Foreign Office. *Documents on British Foreign Policy, 1919–1939*. Edited by E. Llewellyn Woodward and Rohan Butler. 2nd series. 10 vols. to date. London: His Majesty's Stationery Office, 1946–.

Harris, Brice. *The United States and the Italo-Ethiopian Crisis.* Stanford: Stanford University Press, 1964.

Hooker, Nancy Harvison, ed. *The Moffat Papers: Selections from the Diplomatic Journals of Jay Pierrepoint Moffat, 1919–1943.* Cambridge: Harvard University Press, 1956.

Hoover, Herbert. *The Memoirs of Herbert Hoover.* 3 vols. New York: Macmillan Company, 1952.

Hull, Cordell. *The Memoirs of Cordell Hull.* 2 vols. New York: Macmillan Company, 1948.

Jordan, W. M. *Great Britain, France, and the German Problem, 1918–1939.* London: Oxford University Press, 1943.

King, Kenneth L. "The Kellogg-Briand Pact in United States Foreign Policy, 1929–1938." M.A. thesis, Tulane University, 1970.

Link, Arthur S. *American Epoch: A History of the United States Since the 1890's.* 2nd ed. New York: Alfred A. Knopf, 1965.

Literary Digest, 1932–1933.

Morison, Elting E. *Turmoil and Tradition: A Study of the Life and Times of Henry L. Stimson.* Boston: Houghton Mifflin Company, 1960.

Myers, William Starr. *The Foreign Policies of Herbert Hoover, 1929–1933.* New York: Charles Scribner's Sons, 1940.

New York Times, 1932–1933.

O'Connor, Raymond G. *Perilous Equilibrium: The United States and the London Naval Conference of 1930.* Lawrence: University of Kansas Press, 1962.

Pearson, Drew, and Constantine Brown. *The American Diplomatic Game.* Garden City: Doubleday, Doran and Company, 1935.

Pratt, Julius V. *Cordell Hull.* 2 vols. New York: Cooper Square Publishers, 1964.

Rappaport, Armin. *Henry L. Stimson and Japan, 1931–1933.* Chicago: University of Chicago Press, 1963.

Reynolds, P. A. *British Foreign Policy in the Interwar Years.* London: Longmans, Green and Co., 1953.

Smith, Sara R. *The Manchurian Crisis, 1931–1932: A Tragedy in International Relations.* New York: Columbia University Press, 1948.

Stimson, Henry L. "Bases of American Foreign Policy during the Past Four Years." *Foreign Affairs* 11 (April 1933): 383–396.

———. *The Far Eastern Crisis: Recollections and Observations*. New York: Harper and Bros., 1936.

———. Papers. Yale University Library, New Haven, Connecticut.

———, and McGeorge Bundy. *On Active Service in Peace and War*. New York: Harper and Bros., 1947.

The Times (London), 1932–1933.

Toynbee, Arnold J. *Survey of International Affairs, 1932*. London: Oxford University Press, 1933.

———. *Survey of International Affairs, 1933*. London: Oxford University Press, 1934.

United States, Congress, House of Representatives, Committee on Foreign Affairs. *Hearings on the Arms Embargo Resolution of 1933*. Report 22, 73rd Cong., 1st Sess., April 1933. Washington, D.C.: Government Printing Office, 1933.

United States, Department of State. [Henry L. Stimson.] *The Work of the United States Government in the Promotion of Peace during the Past Three Years*. Publication no. 398. Washington, D.C.: Government Printing Office, 1932.

———. *Foreign Relations of the United States: Diplomatic Papers, 1928*. 3 vols. Washington, D.C.: Government Printing Office, 1942–1943.

———. *Foreign Relations of the United States: Diplomatic Papers, 1932*. 5 vols. Washington, D.C.: Government Printing Office, 1947–1948.

———. *Foreign Relations of the United States: Diplomatic Papers, 1933*. 5 vols. Washington, D.C.: Government Printing Office, 1949–1952.

Wheeler-Bennett, John W. *The Disarmament Deadlock*. London: George Routledge and Sons, 1934.

Wolfers, Arnold. *Britain and France between Two Wars: Conflicting Strategies of Peace since Versailles*. New York: Harcourt, Brace and Co., 1940.

Africa: The Kennedy Years, 1961–1963

VAN MITCHELL SMITH

THERE IS AN INHERENT DANGER in the evaluation of American policy toward Africa during the Kennedy years: it is rather too easy to overstate the change that came with the Kennedy period and to see Kennedy as much more of a change from previous leaders than was actually the case. While he saw certain aspects of American foreign policy in a somewhat clearer and certainly different light than his immediate predecessors, his views were, in reality, a combination of the old and the new.

Before the Kennedy years, the long-standing American attitude toward Africa had generally been marked by disinterest. Despite a sentimental concern for the Republic of Liberia, no substantial interests or investments, similar to those in Asia, seemed at stake in Africa. Thus, there was no strong or compelling reason to force the evolution of an American policy toward Africa.

President Cleveland, in 1885, voiced the general American feeling when he expressed opposition to any assumption of responsibility by America "in the remote" valley of the Congo.

During the Boer War, the United States remained neutral, despite widespread sympathy for the Boer cause. Most Americans saw the war from a Boer or British view; there was little or no inclination to consider the feelings of the African majority.[1]

With American involvement in World War I, American concern for Africa grew. However, for the period from 1917 to 1939, American interest remained both minor and sporadic. We continued to view Africa as an appendage of Europe and to see Africa's problems as the colonial concerns of the European powers. Although a tradition of anticolonialism has been an integral part of the American story, this opposition has remained in the realm of philosophy.

Although certain American pronouncements, such as Wilson's Fourteen Points, would have significance in later African developments, and the Africans felt that the concept of self-determination applied to them, this had clearly not been Wilson's intent.

Furthermore, the United States declined any direct role in the mandate system as it was developed in the Wilson-inspired international organization, the League of Nations. The interwar years, 1919 to 1939, saw a continuing "low profile" for America in Africa. Even the American Negro was more concerned with his own domestic problems than he was with the international plight of the "man of color."

When W. E. B. DuBois sought to convene a conference in Paris to bring the plight of the "man of color" before the world, he anticipated the opposition of Wilson and the American delegation. DuBois's view proved correct; the U.S. government declined to issue passports for American blacks to attend. The majority of American Negroes showed only slight inter-

[1] Rupert Emerson, *Africa and United States Policy*, p. 16.

est in this and later Pan-African meetings, although Marcus
Garvey, through his Universal Negro Improvement Association,
foreshadowed a renaissance of the black man in world society.
In fact, many contemporary African and Afro-American leaders
credit Garvey for the revival of a pride in blackness.[2]

American involvement in Liberia grew during the interwar
years as a result of the development of the Firestone holdings
there. A charge of the practice of slavery against Liberia attracted world attention and caused a measure of official em-
barrassment to the U.S. government. There was some American Negro identification with the Ethiopian cause in the
Italo-Ethiopian war,[3] but, in general, America continued to
regard Africa as being of no direct or significant concern to the
United States.

One facet of the interwar years should be noted: there was
an increase in the number of Africans who came to study in
Britain and America. In a sense, this period was an unfortunate
one for such an influx of African students. Ironically, it was
one of the more violent periods of racial strife in our history.
In addition, the economic collapse, the Great Depression of
1929, caused the Western European states and the United States
to narrow their fields of concern to the more personal considerations.

The period of World War II and the subsequent cold war
failed to show any real growth in either American interest or
involvement with Africa. Officially, America continued to see
Africa as the concern of the major colonial powers. We failed
to observe the debilitating effect the war had had on the ability

[2] Kwame Nkrumah, *Ghana: The Autobiography of Kwame Nkrumah*, pp. 45–46.

[3] Ironically, up to this time, the ruling elite of Ethiopia had never
viewed itself as being of Africa or as being black. The acceptance of
African-ness by Ethiopia was to come much later.

of the major European states to continue to discharge their colonial responsibilities. While the concept of decolonization had received rather wide acceptance in England and, to a lesser degree, in France, the United States continued a policy line that often seemed more conservative than that of the colonial powers and cautioned against any premature loosening of colonial ties.

An exception to this American blindness is to be noted in the views of Cordell Hull. He urged America to stand for the progressive attainment of self-government and eventual independence for dependent peoples when they were ready.[4] His principles to guide postwar relationships of the colonial powers with their African and Asian subjects were most far-sighted. They called for a gradual but timed program leading to independence, an effective training program for personnel, and the development of area resources for the local population as well as for the world in general.[5] These principles formed the basis for many of the chapters of the United National Charter that deal with trusteeship and non–self-governing territories. They were a bit too radical for the taste of most colonial powers; they seemed too gradual for the taste of a new generation of African leaders, such as those who dominated the Pan-African Conference at Manchester in 1945.

It should be noted that these principles struck the compromising tone that has continued dominant in much of America's policy toward Africa and toward America's NATO allies. The United States has often sought to cajole its Western allies, at least part of the time, toward some acceptance of a changed relationship toward their colonial peoples, while we have sought to counsel the colonials or the nationalists to be content with a more gradual approach. This approach was evident in the Kennedy years.

[4] Chester Bowles, *Africa's Challenge to America*, p. 109.
[5] Ibid., pp. 109–110.

The Eisenhower-Dulles years were marked by a lamentable
lack of understanding and interest in the colonial problem.
American policy makers during this period saw the world as
neatly divided between good and evil; America and her Western
allies personified the forces of good, while the Communists
stood as the incarnate evil. Dulles, the moralist, saw no zone
between; neutralism, or nonalignment, was a dirty word to him.
If Africa concerned him at all, it was in conjunction with the
cold war and Dulles's desire to prevent Russian penetration of
Africa. Dulles sought a military solution to international problems; he sought the solution in terms of military alliances and
with the concept of a massive retaliatory ability.

The Eisenhower years saw American relations with Africa
dominated by the State Department's Bureau of European Affairs. The following statement accurately characterized the
period: "There was a lack of leadership and a clear articulation
of policy at the pinnacle. He [Kennedy] ended up by saying
that American policymakers must beware of the utopian moral-
ism of Don Quixote and the doubt and vacillation of Hamlet."[6]

As late as 1943, a State Department official, Henry S.
Villard, spoke of Africa as a land with a "relatively primitive
native population." By 1964, American planes were joining
Belgium in air action at Stanleyville. Between those dates, for
three short years, 1961–1963, was an unfortunately brief period
of hope: hope for better American-African understanding.

If one is to examine the Kennedy years, especially with regard
to American policy toward Africa, it is necessary to seek an
understanding of the mind of this young president. Was Kennedy an intellectual? Biographer Arthur Schlesinger, Jr., remarked: "Kennedy was called an intellectual very seldom before
1960 and very often thereafter."[7] Such a statement leads into

[6] Ramesh Sanghvi, *John F. Kennedy: A Political Biography*, p. 108.
[7] Arthur Schlesinger, Jr., *A Thousand Days*, p. 103.

the dangerous region of definition, and each of us may have his own defensible definition. America has had few among its leaders who might properly be styled as intellectuals. Americans have tended to be pragmatic in outlook and have had a built-in suspicion of the intellectual. They have demonstrated a long-standing preference for the "man of action."

A certain dualism can be detected throughout American history, the practical versus the intellectual. Kennedy's efforts were directed toward bringing together once again the world of power and the world of ideas. He saw this not as a new concept but rather as the restoration of a concept that had existed at the time of our nation's creation.

Describing John Kennedy, Schlesinger wrote: "His mind was not prophetic, impassioned, mystical, ontological, utopian or ideological. It was less exuberant than Theodore Roosevelt, less scholarly than Wilson, less adventurous than Franklin Roosevelt. But it had its own salient qualities—it was objective, practical, ironic, unfettered and insatiable."[8] Perhaps in this statement we find the essence of that which we seek, the difference between Kennedy and the leaders who preceded and followed him. This may be the quality that distinguished his administration and its foreign relations from the moralistic guidance of Dulles and the homespun qualities of Lyndon Johnson. Kennedy, in the eyes of some, might not be styled as an intellectual, or, in his own eyes, may not have been one; but he did bring together once again the realms of ideas and action that had distinguished early America. Here may be the true possibilities of American greatness; here may be the essence of the American dream.

Kennedy, like the best historians, combined the analytical and the romantic. He had an uncanny ability to see the views

[8] Ibid.

and motives of those with whom he contended. He did not view the historical struggle as a choice between total good and total evil. His concept of courage for politicians lay in "their acceptance of compromise, through their advocacy of conciliation, and through their willingness to replace conflict with cooperation."[9]

Although deeply aware of human limitations, Kennedy never lost a sense of hope. While he saw history in "its massive movements as shaped by forces beyond man's control," he also believed that many of the world's problems were man-made and were capable of solution by man.[10]

The mind of Kennedy was in essence oriented toward problem solving. He saw with the eyes of the historian rather than the moralist. He always retained an appreciation of the views of others while he defended his own. He was acutely aware of those things over which he felt man had little or no control and those he felt man could and must solve. And he was able to tell the difference.

Kennedy's complex political views derived from a number of sources and experiences. Apart from his formal education, Kennedy gained much from his visits to England during the period his father was ambassador there and from his readings and travels. He began "to perceive the logic and desirability of diverse systems in a diverse world."[11]

Kennedy's life moved him from a sports-oriented school career through a college career that was marked by only erratic evidence of a turning toward the intellectual, through an entrance into politics "as the parochial congressman from Boston,"[12] and through an undistinguished career in the Senate to

[9] Ibid., p. 110.
[10] Ibid., p. 111.
[11] Theodore Sorensen, *The Kennedy Legacy*, p. 26.
[12] Ibid., p. 25.

a short, brilliant, and tragic greatness as president. His friend and biographer, Theodore Sorensen, notes that, in some measure at least, the growth of John F. Kennedy during this period was "simply his own impatient energies reacting to the tedious mediocrity of ideas produced during the sugar-coated Eisenhower years, when nothing went wrong enough for revolution or right enough for celebration."[13]

The emergence of a new and more liberal, more exciting, John Kennedy began to take shape with his visit to Indochina in 1951; however, it was Africa and the Algerian question, as it developed in the mid-fifties, that was to bring him fully to the world stage. His recent selection to the Senate Foreign Relations Committee naturally directed his attention into this channel. With typical Kennedy verve he entered the field of foreign relations with a combination of enthusiasm and careful planning.

At what point he decided to make a major foreign policy speech on the Algerian question in the Senate is not quite clear; it is evident, however, that he began interviewing certain qualified people and gathering materials during the spring of 1957. Kennedy took advantage of the presence of Algerian leaders in New York to meet with them. At the same time, the American secretary of state, Christian Herter, had declined to meet with the Algerian leaders.[14] On July 2, 1957, Kennedy made his Algerian speech, famous to some and infamous to others. From this time forward, his was a voice known to many throughout the world. Indeed, the later favor in which he was to be held by Africans may be said to date from this speech.

Kennedy opened his speech with an attack upon imperialism, both Soviet and Western. He cautioned his listeners that America would be judged on its stand upon "man's desire for free-

13 Ibid., p. 43.
14 Schlesinger, *A Thousand Days*, p. 510.

dom as opposed to a defense of imperialism." He chided
American policy makers for failing to perceive the growing
force of nationalism in Africa. He indicted America's blind and
continuing acceptance of the French position that Algeria was
a domestic problem. He described America's approach to "this
and similar problems as tepid encouragement and moralization
on both sides, cautious neutrality on all real issues, and a re-
statement of our obvious dependence upon our European
friends."[15] He deplored our stand as demonstrating the bank-
ruptcy of our moral leadership in the fight against Soviet
imperialism.[16]

With a perception rare among American statesmen and leaders of the time, Kennedy saw clearly the adverse effect of our
Algerian stand upon our friendship, present and potential, with
the new nations of Africa. He saw how it played into the hands
of anti-Western forces in the Third World. Kennedy condemned the American policy that abandoned African nationalism to those anti-Western forces; he chastised those who labeled
the nationalists and their movements as nothing but communist
fronts.

Having prepared his indictment, Kennedy moved to the advocacy of a more practical, more honest, American program in
Algeria and the rest of Africa. He called on America and France
to abandon the mistakes of the past, to give up wishful thinking over a world that no longer existed, and to face up to the
challenge of an emerging world. He proposed that the United
States give up a policy that abandoned the uncommitted world
of Africa and Asia to the communist and anti-Western elements; he proposed that we offer them a workable American
alternative. However, Kennedy cautioned against panaceas or
intemperate offers of aid. He characterized America's oppor-

[15] John F. Kennedy, *The Strategy of Peace*, p. 69.
[16] Ibid., pp. 68–69.

tunity in Algeria thusly: ". . . in these days, we can help fulfill a great and promising opportunity to show the world that a new nation with an Arab heritage, can establish itself in the western tradition, successfully withstanding both the pull toward Arab feudalism and fanaticism and the pull toward Communist authoritarianism."[17]

His summation was a succinct foreshadowing of the future line of his African views.

If we are to secure the friendship of the Arab, the African and the Asian, we cannot hope to accomplish it solely by means of billion-dollar foreign aid programs. We cannot win their hearts by making them dependent upon our handouts. Nor can we keep them free by selling them free enterprise, by describing the perils of communism or the prosperity of the United States, or limiting our dealings to military pacts. No, the strength of our appeal to these key populations lies in our traditional and deeply felt philosophy of freedom and independence for all peoples everywhere.[18]

Although the speech was to bring Kennedy world-wide notice, the response in the United States and Western Europe was mainly adverse. The speech produced great irritation in official circles in both Washington and Paris. Many observers, including some Democrats, felt that by criticizing a long-time ally, France, Kennedy had threatened the future of the Western alliance. Even so staunch a liberal as Adlai Stevenson felt that Kennedy had gone too far in his remarks.[19]

Soon after making this speech, Kennedy became chairman of the Subcommittee on Africa of the Senate Foreign Relations Committee.

In this capacity, he warned his colleagues about the new energies bursting forth in the dark continent [Schlesinger's choice of words].

[17] Ibid., p. 75.
[18] Ibid., pp. 79–80.
[19] Schlesinger, *A Thousand Days*, pp. 510–511.

"Call it nationalism, call it anti-colonialism, call it what you will," he said in 1959, "Africa is going through a revolution . . . The word is out and spreading like wildfire in nearly a thousand languages and dialects—that it is no longer necessary to remain forever in bondage." He advocated sympathy with the independence movement, programs of economic and education assistance, and as a goal of American policy, "a strong Africa."[20]

The presidential election of 1960 had at least one unique feature; for the first time, American policy toward Africa, and especially the emergent nations of Africa and their leaders, became a significant campaign point. Also, for the first time, the office was sought by a man who was willing to view Africa and her problems in a new and independent light. In the campaign, Kennedy repeatedly pointed out that "we have lost ground in Africa because we have neglected and ignored the needs and aspirations of the African People."[21]

In building his campaign, Kennedy turned to a group of "academic advisers" for expert advice in such areas as foreign policy, economics, military affairs, housing, and urban planning. This group did much to improve Kennedy's image with American liberals. The advisers also provided much material for position papers and campaign speeches, as well as information that formed the basis of the legislative programs of the early Kennedy period.

Facing the young president-elect was both the drafting of the program and the selection of aides to carry out the new directions he seemed determined to embark upon. The concerns of this study are primarily with those aspects of the program of the "New Frontier" that might alter the direction of American foreign policy and might introduce new and more imaginative outlooks with regard to such areas in Africa. Patrick Anderson

20 Ibid., p. 511.
21 Ibid.

wrote of John Kennedy: " . . . not since Roosevelt had there been a president so distrustful of the bureaucracy and so willing to let his personal aides prod, double-check and by-pass it."[22]

Out of the task of staffing the upper levels of the State Department came the emergence of the "little State Department" within the White House under McGeorge Bundy. Kennedy had wanted both McGeorge Bundy and Walt Rostow in high posts in the State Department. However, Rusk resisted such appointments for both of these men. "From the institutional interests of the Department this was a grievous error. Kennedy promptly decided to take them into the White House, Bundy as a Special Assistant for National Security Affairs and Rostow as his deputy. The result was to give the White House an infusion of energy in foreign affairs with which the State Department would never in the next three years quite catch up."[23]

In the job of building his team for the "New Frontier," Kennedy, as always, sought to combine ideas with practical considerations. While he was always fascinated and stimulated by new ideas and by challenging concepts, Kennedy was at the same time the realist, the practical politician. Therefore, his selection process included a formula for seeking a balance between the two. He realized that the men who were chosen must be able to translate philosophies into practical actions; they must be chosen, of course, for their general ability, but also for their ability to function within the establishment. In keeping with his conviction that more could be changed by compromise and persuasion than by confrontation, he passed over certain able men for important posts on his team. He felt that they were too controversial.

Complicating the foreign policy picture for the incoming Kennedy administration was a sharp division among Democratic

[22] Sorensen, *The Kennedy Legacy,* p. 63.
[23] Schlesinger, *A Thousand Days,* pp. 144–145.

foreign policy strategists. One school of thought, led by Dean Acheson, was military centered and Europe oriented. "Acheson's ideas had grown out of his own brilliant period as Secretary of State, when the Soviet Union first became a nuclear power, a disorganized Western Europe lay under the Soviet guns and the Communists were attempting direct aggression in Korea. Those years had demanded, above all, a revival of military will and power in the West."[24] A decade later, his views on American foreign policy had not changed. "He was increasingly concerned lest the United States allow herself to be diverted from the main battleground of Europe into sentimental crusades against colonialism and hopeless efforts to democratize the underdeveloped world."[25]

The rival school, led by Adlai Stevenson and supported by Averell Harriman, George Kennan, Chester Bowles, G. Mennen Williams, J. K. Galbraith, J. William Fulbright, and Mike Mansfield, believed in the concept of a radically changed world. They believed "that the military threat to Western Europe had receded, that the underdeveloped world was the new battleground, and military measures had to be supplemented, not superceded, by vigorous political and economic programs."[26] Though Kennedy tried to stay out of the quarrels between the Democratic Advisory Committee members, his views, evidenced as early as 1957 by his Algerian speech, fitted more clearly the latter of the two groups, the Stevenson, rather than the Acheson, group.

Fundamental to the Kennedy view were the ideas given in his State of the Union address in January 1962. Then he said, ". . . our basic goal remains the same; a peaceful world community of free and independent nations, free to choose their

24 Ibid., p. 280.
25 Ibid.
26 Ibid., pp. 280–281.

own future and their own system so long as it does not threaten the freedom of others."[27] He projected an American foreign relations posture that drew from "five strengths: the moral and physical strength of the United States; the united strength of the Atlantic community; the regional strength of the Americas; the creative strength of our efforts in the new and developing nations; the peace keeping strength of the United Nations."[28]

Possibly the best statement of John F. Kennedy's view of foreign policy came in a commencement address at American University on June 10, 1963. He opened with a definition of peace: not a Pax Americana but a peace for all men.[29] Drawing upon his own long-standing dislike and distrust of the military solution, he advocated the pursuit of peace with the same tenacity with which men had pursued war.

He urged upon his listeners a more realistic view of American-Russian relations. With his known penchant for trying to see the point of view of others, he cautioned his audience to avoid finding total fault in the Russians and total virtue in themselves. Kennedy believed that the United States might assist Russian leadership to what he called "a more enlightened attitude" toward world relations. He called for a peace of realism, not of utopian lines. As always, he sought the middle ground, the route of compromise. He came again to a favored theme: "And if we cannot end now our differences, at least we can help make the world safe for diversity."[30]

Of the many appointments to be made, the filling of the post of secretary of state was among the most difficult. While he was still pondering this appointment, Kennedy demonstrated his

[27] President Kennedy, "State of the Union Message," *Department of State Bulletin*, January 29, 1962, p. 159.

[28] Ibid.

[29] President Kennedy, "The Strategy of Peace," in *Vital Speeches*, vol. 29, p. 558.

[30] Ibid., p. 559.

feelings on Africa by naming G. Mennen Williams to the post of assistant secretary of state for African affairs. While there was considerable comment, much of it amused in tone, over Williams's appointment, it was viewed by others, including many Africans, as evidence that the new Kennedy administration was seeking an independent approach for America's African policies. Also significant for Africa was the appointment of Chester Bowles as undersecretary of state.

Complicating the picture for the incoming Kennedy administration was the staffing of field posts in Africa. Outgoing Deputy Undersecretary Loy Henderson's plan to staff these posts with senior service officers was unearthed by members of the Kennedy team. A Kennedy aide, Thomas Farmer, opposed the plan on the grounds that such posts should not go to tired old men awaiting their pensions but to young officers with careers to make, or even to people outside the Foreign Service.[31]

Earlier in June of 1960, before becoming president, Kennedy outlined a foreign policy for Africa, saying:

We must greatly increase our efforts to encourage the newly emerging nations of the vast continent of Africa—to persuade them that they do not have to turn to Moscow for the guidance or friendship they so desperately need . . . We can no longer afford policies which refuse to accept the inevitable triumph of nationalism in Africa—the inevitable end of colonialism . . . And finally, if our policies toward Africa are to be effective, we must extend this [economic] aid in terms of America's desire to bring freedom and prosperity to Africa— not in terms of narrow self-interest which seeks to use African nations as pawns in the cold war.[32]

It is likely that John Kennedy made his most significant contribution in the field of personal diplomacy. While African

[31] Schlesinger, *A Thousand Days*, p. 145.
[32] Kennedy, *The Strategy of Peace*, unnumbered insert by the publisher.

leaders often arrived at the White House proud, tense, unsure, Kennedy melted their reserve with a warm and casual charm. He showed a knowledge of Africa and an understanding of African nationalism they had not anticipated. He accepted non-alignment, or neutralism, as a proper African position. He met them as equal partners, not as a patronizing or superior figure. He invited their views, saw their problems, and asked only their appreciation of the intricacy of his problems. As his own molder of American policy in Africa, Kennedy sought to convert his African guests to a more favorable view of the United States. He sought to demonstrate to them, in positive terms, a comparison between the American and Communist ways.

Three major figures created Kennedy's African policy: Kennedy, Chester Bowles, and G. Mennen Williams. Others, such as Adlai Stevenson, guided American policy through the often treacherous currents of U.N. politics—steering between the views and wishes of our NATO allies and the expectations and hopes of the new nations of Africa and the rest of the developing world.

Of the framers of Kennedy's African policy, the thoughts and views of Chester Bowles are second in importance only to those of the president himself. In a speech in December 1962, Bowles sketched in the lines of an American program for Africa. He asked the question: ". . . how should the United States deal with the new Africa? The first requirement, it seems to me, is to continue to make everlastingly clear our support for the right of all people to determine their own form of government."[33] He urged upon his listeners the need of appreciating, at the same time, the real difficulties that were facing our European friends. He advocated an aid program for Africa that was realistic, one that was designed to meet the needs of the

[33] Chester Bowles, "A Close Look at Africa," *Department of State Bulletin*, December 31, 1962, pp. 1005–1006.

African states and that was capable of being absorbed by the existing resources of such states. Wisely, he noted, ". . . in our desire to build a partnership with the African nations, let us be careful not to compromise our interests or principles in an effort to please them on short-term issues where we feel in all honesty that they are in error."[34] He concluded with a thought that the new African states, understandably, just having escaped from the confinement of colonialism, were not likely to accept Russianization, Sinicization, or Americanization. They would accept only Africanization.

An expanded presentation of Bowles's long interest in and thoughts upon Africa and American relations with Africa may be found in his earlier work, written in 1956, *Africa's Challenge to America*. It was only a year after the publication of this work that Kennedy made his Algerian speech. Many of Bowles's ideas would find their way into the "New Frontier."

Another spokesman for the "New Frontier" was G. Mennen Williams. It is more as a communicator than as a policy maker that Williams made his contribution. Derisively referred to by his critics as "Soapy," he nevertheless made an effective spokesman in Africa for Kennedy's policy. While his famous Nairobi remark, "Africa for Africans," angered African whites, Europeans, and many Americans, it made friends among black Africans.

Williams summarized his concept of an American policy toward Africa in this manner:

Our African policy has five major points. *First*, and most importantly, we support self-determination for Africa and all corollaries that follow from it, such as the African desire for non-alignment.
Second, we encourage the Africans themselves to solve their own problems. We support without reservations those institutions through

[34] Ibid.

which Africans can arrive at their own solutions, like the Organization of African Unity and the U.N. Economic Commission for Africa. *Third*, we hope to raise the African standard of living with our aid and our trade.

Fourth, we discourage the build-up of arms beyond the needs of internal security of legitimate self-defense.

Fifth, we remind other countries, particularly the European metropoles, of their continuing responsibilities toward Africa.[35]

In developing the American program for Africa, Williams noted that the new nations should avoid an independent status that carried forward an exclusive relationship with the former colonial power. In this observation, he warned against the status that the Africans would come to call *neocolonialism*. He believed that the United States could help the new nations' sense of independence by offering them an alternate "great power" relationship.[36]

Others were significant in expanding American policies and programs for Africa. Among those were Adlai Stevenson, from his post as ambassador to the United Nations; George Ball, in the delicate area of NATO versus the developing nations; Wayne Fredericks; and George McGhee.

The Kennedy policy toward Africa was a skilful combination of the old and the new. It has been previously noted that Kennedy liked to combine the realm of ideas with the realm of performance. During my own visits to Africa, various Africans remarked to me that they did not question our ability to write and enunciate great ideas, but they did doubt our ability to live great concepts. Therefore, let us ask ourselves, did the actions and reactions of Kennedy reflect the policy statements or did he say one thing and do quite another? Let us examine some of the events that occurred in Africa, 1961–1963: the crises in

[35] G. Mennen Williams, *Africa for the Africans*, p. 170.
[36] Ibid., p. 176.

Algeria, the Congo, South Africa and Southwest Africa, Portuguese Africa, Ghana and the Volta River project, and Guinea.

Against the backdrop of Kennedy's 1957 Algerian speech, Algeria was to furnish the Kennedy administration a real test. As the Algerian conflict moved toward another crisis, the United States found its previous close association with France as well as its good relations with the independent governments of Morocco and Tunisia threatened.

While the United States and the rest of the world watched the efforts of de Gaulle to bring a settlement in Algeria by talks with the nationalist leaders, the pro-Western leader in Tunisia, President Bourguiba, produced a new crisis for the United States. He demanded the French withdrawal from the base at Bizerte. The United States faced the threat of weakening the Atlantic alliance if she offended France; however, by siding with France, she would arouse anticolonial feeling throughout the world.

In the face of Soviet support for Bourguiba's action, the United States tried a moderate position and abstained on an African-supported resolution. There appeared to be an inconsistency in the U.S. position. During the debate before the U.N. vote, Stevenson supported this resolution; however, on the vote, he abstained. Behind the scene, direct action by Kennedy altered the American stand. According to Schlesinger, Kennedy's advice was as follows: "Everyone forgets how shaky de Gaulle's position is . . . if the Tunisian affair goes really sour, it might start a new military revolt. We don't want the 'ultras' to take over France. With all his faults the General is the best hope for a solution in Algeria. Tell Adlai that our sympathy is with the anti-colonial nations; but their cause won't be helped by the over-throw of de Gaulle, nor will our position in Berlin. Let's sit this one out."[37] Having appeared to be "in the French camp"

37 Schlesinger, *A Thousand Days*, p. 518.

on this crucial vote, Kennedy asked the State Department to prepare a letter to Bourguiba. On the final draft of that letter, Kennedy wrote: "Standing as my country does—close to a holocaust that could destroy the U.S. as well as Europe and much of the East, I have not found it possible to take a public position on this matter satisfactory with you. I regret this greatly, but I am hopeful that you will recognize our difficulties as well as those of your country in these days."[38] The situation moved once more toward solution with the resumption of French-Algerian talks. A settlement was announced May 18, 1962. It was hailed by the United States as a "historic accomplishment made possible by vision, statesmanship, and moderation of all concerned."[39]

Had Kennedy's administration worked for an Algerian solution that reflected the views of his 1957 Senate speech or was the solution a break from this earlier stand? It would appear that Kennedy tried to combine the realm of philosophy with the realm of reality in the solution. It portrayed his concept of the "courage of compromise."

The Kennedy policy may well have received its most severe challenge and criticism in the Congo. The Congolese crisis was a crisis not only for the Congo and the United States, but also for all nations of the world, in and out of the United Nations, and especially for the young nations of Africa.

Only a month in office, Kennedy issued a special statement on the Congo, on February 15: " 'The United Nations offers the best, if not the only, possibility for the restoration of stability and order in the Congo.' He went on to warn, in view of violence in Moscow's recent statements, that the United States would feel obligated 'to defend the character of the U.N. by

[38] Ibid.
[39] Richard P. Stebbins, *The United States in World Affairs, 1962*, p. 237.

opposing any attempt by any government to intervene uni-
laterally in the Congo.' "[40] In addition to support of the role
of the United Nations in the Congo, the Kennedy policy in the
Congo worked, through Ambassador Edmund Gullion, to effect
a reconciliation by negotiation between Tshombe of Katanga
and the central Congo government. This American effort came
under severe attack both at home and abroad. A sizeable bloc
of conservative Americans, as well as a significant bloc of world
opinion, looked on Tshombe as the only true anticommunist
among the Congo leaders. In addition, his attitude toward foreign business won him many friends. Several of America's prin-
cipal allies had grave misgivings over the apparently increasing
willingness of the Kennedy administration to support a U.N.
takeover of Katanga, even by military means, if deemed necessary. Ambassador Gullion played a pivotal role in negotiations
that led to the Kitona agreement between the central government and Tshombe. Assurance from U Thant against the "use
of force" secured British and Belgian, in addition to American,
support to the agreement. However, U Thant's plan for economic sanctions received scant support.

In spite of assurances by the U.N. secretary-general, the
answer to the Katanga question veered increasingly toward
military conflict. From the point of view of the central Congo
government, backed by the majority of the African states, the
end of the secession "would represent an important victory for
the principle of national independence and integrity in emergent
Africa."[41] The United States continued support of the United
Nations and the secretary-general and even agreed to military
action. It was the U.S. State Department's attitude that the secession must be ended if the central government authority was

[40] Ibid., p. 254.
[41] Ibid., p. 250.

ever to be secured and the fear of Communist intervention was to be ended.[42]

January 21, 1963, saw U.N. forces enter Kolwezi, a mining center and the last Tshombe stronghold; the secession was over. "The right or wrong" of the U.N. policy was, in a sense, answered by its success.

Kennedy's Congo policy is still controversial. Was the United States right in its decision to back a U.N. solution, even a military one, in the Congo? Was the policy consistent with the general lines of his African program? It would appear that Kennedy and his advisers saw the central Congo government as the only alternative to "balkanization" of the Congo and, possibly, to unilateral Russian intervention in the area. It was believed that Soviet intervention would produce a "cold war" confrontation between the super-powers for the support of the African governments and the people. Kennedy preferred to prevent such an occurrence and seek a peaceful, competitive presentation of the two philosophies to the African states and peoples. His Congo policy, therefore, appears consistent with such a goal. One note of failure is apparent with regard to the post-secession Congo; an effective program of economic aid and rehabilitation did not materialize.

The Portuguese colonies, or, as the Portuguese insist on calling them, overseas provinces, presented the Kennedy administration with still another delicate African problem. The outbreak of serious unrest in Angola brought world attention to Portugal's African territories. A U.N. resolution, sponsored by Liberia, called on the Security Council to make an inquiry into the Angolan situation; it also contained a veiled warning to Portugal to begin reforming her African territories. Portugal, was of no concern to the United Nations. In the resulting dis-

---

[42] *Department of State Bulletin*, February 4, 1963, pp. 165–170.

of course, contended that the matter was domestic in nature and cussion, the United States, acting under the president's direction, left its NATO allies and voted with the USSR and three Asian and African members of the council.[43]

The United States sought to dissuade the African states from harsh aggressive actions against Portugal through unsupportable resolutions and unenforceable policies while, at the same time, the United States sought to persuade Portugal to accept what seemed to represent the "wave of the future." Generally, Kennedy's stand resulted in feelings of hostility toward the United States from both sides. The African states felt that the United States was too concerned over its NATO friends to stand forthright with the Africans. Portugal felt that the United States was meddling in a Portuguese domestic affair. While the U.S. policy was consistent with Kennedy's thinking, it was much less successful than his Congo policy.

On the matter of South Africa, too, the Kennedy administration was confronted with much division of opinion, even within the United States. In the spring of 1961, Ghana and the bulk of the African states confronted the U.N. Assembly with a new and more strident demand with regard to white-dominated South Africa. They were no longer willing to accept mere resolutions of opinions; they now called for definite political and economic sanctions, for the severance of diplomatic relations, and for trade embargoes against South Africa.

While the United States was not a defender of the racial policies of South Africa toward its nonwhite population, it felt that the application of sanctions would only stiffen the will of the Afrikaner and worsen the lot of the Africans in the republic. American policy toward South Africa was further complicated by substantial American financial involvement in South Africa

[43] *Department of State Bulletin*, April 3, 1961, vol. 44, pp. 497–499.

Liberal American thought joined the African in the view that American policy was based more on financial and business involvement than on the historic principles of American political philosophy.

American policy toward the question of Southwest Africa, in support of the African position on a 1961 resolution, was a source of both surprise and gratification to the Africans. Although U.S. policy subsequently returned to an advocacy of persuasion over force in the matter, it continued a policy largely acceptable to at least moderate African opinion. By 1962, however, there was a definite trend toward a more aggressive stand by the African states; American and British views for persuasion over force were increasingly less convincing to the Africans. A Ghana-inspired resolution of 1962 is illustrative of the new African mood. It called on "all U.N. members to break off diplomatic relations with South Africa, and, in addition, asked the Security Council to consider the expelling of South Africa unless its policy was altered."[44]

While the effect of the resolution was slight, as the main opponents of the boycott were South Africa's best customers, the action brought the argument into sharper focus than ever.

American policy in regard to South Africa won few friends. Although consistent with Kennedy's view of moderation, it was successful neither in tempering the aggressiveness of the African states nor in arousing the moral consciousness of the white South Africans.

Only two additional Kennedy actions with regard to Africa will be noted: his policy toward Sekou Touré of Guinea, and the question of Ghana and American involvement in the financing of the Volta River project.

The Eisenhower administration had written Guinea off as lost

[44] Stebbins, *The United States in World Affairs, 1962*, p. 266.

to the Communist bloc.[45] Kennedy took another view. The fascination with the break-up of the French Empire, as well as a desire to meet the man who had said "no" to de Gaulle, led him in 1959 to seek out Touré when the Guinean leader visited the United States.[46] During the 1960 campaign, Kennedy criticized the eight-month delay of the American government in dispatching an ambassador to Guinea. He asserted that "today Guinea has moved toward the Communist bloc because of our neglect."[47]

Kennedy's appointment of William Attwood as American ambassador to Guinea was accompanied by instructions to the new envoy that he ascertain the correctness of Kennedy's belief that Sekou Touré still remained at heart a nationalist. Attwood's findings agreed with the president's belief and formed the basis for an accelerated aid program and a most successful visit to Guinea by Sargent Shriver. Because the anti-American tone of Touré and Guinea changed abruptly during a visit to the United Nations of the Guinean leader in 1962, Kennedy invited him to visit Washington.

On returning to Guinea, Touré said, "At the end of our talks with President Kennedy, I and the Guinean delegation expressed our satisfaction to have found in the United States President a man quite open to African problems and determined to promote the American contribution to their happy solution."[48]

In the case of American relations with Ghana, the Kennedy administration inherited a tense-to-openly-hostile situation. In September 1960 the American secretary of state, Christian Herter, had caused a hostile reaction from Ghana by his re-

[45] Schlesinger, *A Thousand Days*, pp. 523–524.
[46] Ibid., p. 529.
[47] Ibid.
[48] Ibid., p. 525.

mark that Nkrumah was "very definitely moving toward the Soviet bloc."[49]

The question of American financial involvement in the building of a hydroelectric dam on the Volta River was still a moot point; however, in light of the steady deterioration of Ghana-U.S. relations, the project appeared to have slight chance of being carried out. Barbara Ward, the British economist, urged Kennedy to reconsider the matter. As he had great respect for Barbara Ward, Kennedy felt strengthened in his favorable view toward the project. Nkrumah was invited to the White House in March 1961. "The visit was a success. The Kennedys liked him, and Nkrumah was so moved that on the plane back to New York he scrawled Kennedy a warm personal note . . . expressing his pleasure at the meeting and his hope for future friendship."[50]

For the moment, the visit appeared to be a triumph for the Kennedy charm and his style of personal African diplomacy. In July, Kennedy wrote affirming U.S. intentions to participate in the Volta project. In the subsequent months, however, Nkrumah's exercises in what he called "positive neutrality" appeared, even to President Kennedy, increasingly pro Communist. Kennedy began to waver on the Volta project. He received a query from his father: " 'What in the hell are you up to with that Communist Nkrumah?' . . . The President well understood that cancellation of the Volta Dam now would set back his whole African policy, while support would dramatize the new American attitude toward non-alignment throughout Africa. He hoped that this policy would preserve a positive American presence within Ghana and that Nkrumah's national-

[49] Ibid., p. 526.
[50] Ibid., p. 527.

ism would in the end prevail over his leanings toward the East."[51]

Although Kennedy viewed with grave misgivings the continuing drift of Nkrumah to the East, he held on to his view that the Volta project should be seen as an act for Ghana, not for Nkrumah.

Throughout the Kennedy years, 1961–1963, and in the specific cases examined above, one can observe Kennedy's consistent approach to Africa. In all, he tried the diplomacy of moderation and compromise. He sought to find a middle course more aggressive than his Western allies might prefer, more moderate than his African friends might wish. He sought a policy that both might be persuaded to accept. He did not ask the African to align himself irrevocably with the West. He accepted nonalignment as proper foreign policy stance for Africa, and he accepted the African's desire to stand aside from the involvement in the cold war. Kennedy believed that Dulles's approach of military intervention would bear less fruit than the demonstration of the virtues of democracy to the African. He abandoned the military approach of Dulles for the advocacy of a competitive presentation of democracy versus communism to Africa.

Though Kennedy is still remembered in Africa, in the final analysis, his interest in Africa and his American program for Africa did not reflect the majority of American thinking. Under his successors, Johnson and Nixon, American policy moved back toward the majority's thinking, toward a European orientation. American concern over and involvement in Africa grew less; there was no dynamic young American president, knowledgeable in African affairs, to exert his charisma over visiting African leaders.

[51] Ibid., pp. 528–529.

Of course, in fairness to his successors, the shadow of American involvement in Vietnam troubled our relations with the African states and our relations with most of the rest of the world.

As the magazine *West Africa* later put it, the Africans "considered that Mr. Kennedy's political attitudes were even more important than his efforts to aid their economies."[52] With his death, the Africans felt that they had lost a true friend; they were right.

[52] Ibid., p. 514.

BIBLIOGRAPHY

Bowles, Chester. *Africa's Challenge to America.* Berkeley: University of California Press, 1956.

Emerson, Rupert. *Africa and United States Policy.* Englewood Cliffs, N.J.: Prentice-Hall, 1967.

Kennedy, John F. *The Strategy of Peace.* Edited by Allan Nevins. New York: Harper & Row, Publishers, 1962.

Nkrumah, Kwame. *Ghana: The Autobiography of Kwame Nkrumah.* New York: Thomas Nelson and Sons, 1957.

Sanghvi, Ramesh. *John F. Kennedy: A Political Biography.* Bombay: Perennial Press, 1961.

Schlesinger, Arthur, Jr. *A Thousand Days.* New York: Fawcett World Library, 1967.

Sorensen, Theodore. *The Kennedy Legacy.* New York: New American Library, 1970.

Stebbins, Richard P., ed. *The United States in World Affairs, 1961.* New York: Harper & Row, Publishers, 1962.

————. *The United States in World Affairs, 1962.* New York: Harper & Row, Publishers, 1963.

————. *The United States in World Affairs, 1963.* New York: Harper & Row, Publishers, 1964.

United States, Department of State, *Bulletin.* Vols. 44–48, 1961–1963.

Vital Speeches. Vol. 29, October 1962–October 1963.

Williams, G. Mennen. *Africa for the Africans.* Grand Rapids: William B. Erdman Publishing Co., 1969.

The Roots of Conflict
Soviet Images in the American Press, 1941–1947

☒☒

ELLIOTT WEST

GENERAL SHERMAN THOUGHT WAR was hell. But American historians often seem closest to paradise when arguing about the half dozen or so major conflicts of our past. Recently the Second World War and the cold war that followed have attracted special scholarly attention. In particular, many students have analyzed the relations between the United States and the Soviet Union during World War II, while others have debated why that strange alliance collapsed during the years after 1945. By the traditional view, the United States sought to keep alive its wartime cooperation with the USSR but finally had to take its stand against the ambitions of Soviet Russia. Revisionists, however, have placed the burden of guilt not on the Soviet Union but on our government, which supposedly provoked Stalin's hostility by a policy of economic aggression.[1]

[1] The term "revisionist" here refers to historians who emphasize the desire of the United States to expand its economic influence, especially into east Europe, as the prime precipitating factor of the cold war. Sev-

Diplomatic developments during the crucial years of 1941–1947 have been studied in bewildering detail. Yet one aspect of the story, the attitudes of the American people toward the Soviet Union, remains neglected. When writers touch on this subject at all, they usually emphasize the wartime public's feelings of fellowship for Soviet Russia, a "reservoir of goodwill" which gradually ran dry as the cold war began.[2] In 1945 we supposedly stood, hat in hand, on the doorstep of Joseph Stalin as an ardent suitor for the hand of Russia, only to find that the object of our affections wanted not to spoon but to spat.

However, to understand fully the relations between the Soviet and U.S. governments, we must take a closer look at this cliché. If public opinion usually is vague and contradictory, it always has helped define the parameters of this country's diplomatic policies. These years were no exception. How our government acted toward the Soviet Union depended partly on what Americans thought about the leaders and society of the USSR. A brief survey of some of the most widely read newspapers and magazines can provide a few impressions, however crude, of the clusters of attitudes that formed the public's images of Soviet Russia. Such a study suggests that the apparent popular friend-

---

eral helpful historiographical surveys of this debate have been published: John Snell, "The Cold War: Four Contemporary Appraisals," *American Historical Review* 68 (October 1962): 69–75; Norman A. Graebner, "Cold War Origins and the Contemporary Debate," *Journal of Conflict Resolution* 13 (March 1969): 123–132; Paul Seabury, "Cold War Origins, I," *Journal of Contemporary History* 3 (January 1968): 169–182; Brian Thomas, "Cold War Origins, II," *Journal of Contemporary History* 3 (January 1968): 183–198; Henry Pachter, "Revisionist Historians and the Cold War," *Dissent* 15 (November 1968): 505–518; Christopher Lasch, "The Cold War Revisited and Revisioned," *New York Times Magazine*, January 14, 1968, pp. 26–27, 44–59.

[2] The quoted phrase is from John W. Spanier, *American Foreign Policy since World War II*, p. 27.

ship toward Russia was more complex and more fragile than usually is recalled.

As the year 1941 began, the American press regarded the Soviet Union with a hostility rarely matched before or since. During the previous four years, the purge trials and evidence of official terror had painted an alarming picture of a police state under Stalin's rule. Above all, the Russo-German nonaggression pact of August 1939 turned popular opinion against Russia with dramatic suddenness by opening the way for Hitler's *Wehrmacht* to invade Poland and plunge Europe into war. During the months that followed, the Soviet assaults on Poland and the Baltic states and the invasion of Finland deepened still further the public's antagonism.[3]

In fact, this quick succession of events triggered an anti-Soviet reaction reminiscent of the wildest hysteria of the Red Scare. As Hollywood stars performed in benefits for the fighting Finns, the Cambridge, Massachusetts, city council banned the words "Lenin" and "Leningrad" from school texts and atlases.[4] In this atmosphere the image of the Soviet Union merged with that of the other scourge of Europe, Nazi Germany. "Now when Fascist and Communist clasp hands, lie down together and swear eternal fealty one to the other, the truth becomes clear,"

[3] Two treatments of earlier attitudes toward the Soviet Union provide a background for this period: Peter G. Filene, *Americans and the Soviet Experiment, 1917–1933*, and Frank A. Warren III, *Liberals and Communism: The "Red Decade" Revisited*. For examples of public hostility after August 1939, see Robert Sobel, *The Origins of Interventionism: The United States and the Russo-Finnish War*, pp. 109–117; Donald O. Dewey, "America and Russia 1939–1941: The Views of the New York Times," *Journalism Quarterly* 44 (Spring 1967): 62–70; *New York Herald Tribune*, December 3, 1939, p. 3; *Denver Post*, December 1, 1939, p. 2.

[4] *Saturday Evening Post*, March 16, 1940, p. 28; *Denver Post*, December 27, 1939, p. 2.

wrote Ralph McGill of the *Atlanta Constitution.* "Only in name
are they different."[5] Ideological distinctions between national
socialism and communism blurred, while Adolf Hitler and
Joseph Stalin both appeared in the press as international rene-
gades who, as the *Wall Street Journal* put it, differed only in
the length of their respective mustaches.[6]

Then, on June 22, 1941, the scene changed again. When
Hitler abruptly turned upon his Russian ally and launched an
invasion along an eighteen-hundred-mile front, both British
Prime Minister Winston Churchill and President Franklin
Roosevelt quickly saw the wisdom of offering their aid to Mar-
shal Stalin in a common conflict against Nazidom. Most editors
also recognized the need to support the USSR to weaken the
German war machine. At the same time, however, they reaffirmed their opinion that the Soviet and Nazi regimes were little
different in their beliefs and policies.[7] Germany was the most immediate menace to Western values and society, the editors of the
San Francisco Chronicle believed, and any foe of Hitler should receive our help. Yet the *Chronicle* also advised American leaders
to "walk warily" in Soviet relations and in a scant six inches of
copy managed to describe Stalin as stupid, treacherous, idiotic,
calloused, tyrannical, power mad, and loutish.[8]

Only the Japanese attack on Pearl Harbor opened the way for
a deeper change in the public's attitude toward Soviet Russia. As
the United States moved from the periphery to the vortex of

5 *Atlanta Constitution,* January 5, 1940, p. 8.

6 *New York Herald Tribune,* December 1, 1939, p. 24. *Wall Street
Journal* quoted in Les K. Adler and Thomas G. Patterson, "Red Fascism: The Merger of Nazi Germany and Soviet Russia in the American
Image of Totalitarianism, 1930's–1950's," *American Historical Review*
75 (April 1970): 1049–1064.

7 For a survey of press opinion during this period, see Raymond H.
Dawson, *The Decision to Aid Russia, 1941: Foreign and Domestic Politics,* Chapter 4.

8 *San Francisco Chronicle,* June 24, 1941, p. 12; July 18, 1941, p. 14.

the conflict, its new role demanded the total spiritual commitment of the American people. But here a problem arose, for an
ally of tainted and dubious character, such as Russia, could
prove to be a dangerous psychological barrier to an all-out effort
for victory. The war seemed to demand that our comrades in
arms be portrayed in the best possible light—and that included
the Soviet bear so recently condemned as hopelessly depraved.
Under these circumstances, readers of the popular press witnessed
nothing less than the creation of a new Russia. Aspects of
Soviet life criticized earlier now appeared to be changing for
the better, while many editors optimistically predicted an era
of postwar cooperation as Soviet diplomats abandoned dreams
of expansion. Gradually, the rough edges of the Russian image
were smoothed away, and the reading public saw the Soviet
Union remade to fit the mold of American ideals.

Of all facets of Russian life, none appeared more worthy of
admiration than the Red Army. At precisely that time when
Americans were committing themselves to world war, the Soviet
Union was inflicting the first serious setbacks upon German
forces. As the ungracious Russian winter of 1941–1942 stalled
Hitler's three-pronged attack, correspondents like Eve Curie and
C. L. Sulzberger told the public of a determined, well-organized
defense by an army of brave and patriotic young men.[9] Many
editors who had anticipated an early Soviet defeat now offered
open praise for such resistance, and one columnist went so far
as to propose a national "Russia-You-Made-A-Bunch-Of-
Monkeys-Out-Of-Us-Week."[10] Commendation could be heard

[9] C. L. Sulzberger, "Sergei, Red Fighter," New York Times Magazine, January 4, 1942, pp. 4, 23; Eve Curie, "Reds Determined," Dallas
Morning News, January 8, 1942, sec. 2, p. 3. Eve Curie, daughter of
physicists Pierre and Marie Curie, was a war correspondent following
the fall of France.

[10] Henry McLemore, "Brave Russia," Dallas Morning News, January
26, 1942, sec. 2, p. 3.

far different in both tone and volume from the critical support
of the previous fall. In February 1942, for instance, General
Douglas MacArthur advised the American public that "the
hopes of civilization rest on the worthy banners of the coura-
geous Russian army."[11] Clearly this nation had gone far toward
unanimous praise of the Soviet military.

Behind the Red Army, the public was told, stood the equally
valiant and martial Russian people. Self-sacrificing, slow to
anger but implacable in battle, the Soviet citizen was held up to
the American reader as an example of wartime dedication.
Newspaper and magazine columns abounded with descriptions
of Moscow's children filling sandbags and training with rifles
and grenades, while other writers praised the men and women
who worked hours overtime constructing the defenses of their
homeland.[12] Visual images helped humanize Americans' view
of Russian life. Just as movies like *North Star* and *Song of
Russia* sentimentalized Soviet wartime travails, the photographic
essays of *Collier's* magazine portrayed sympathetically the harsh
everyday lot of peasant and city dweller.[13] Middle America's
window to exotic lands, *National Geographic Magazine*, featured glossy color photos of grinning farmers, buxom girls, and
charming, round-faced babies of the Caucasus and Volga valley.
Even the climate, like the populace, was presented in a more
agreeable light—one article was entitled "Sunny Siberia."[14]

[11] *Los Angeles Times*, February 24, 1942, p. 4; *Boston Globe*, April
21, 1944, p. 18. MacArthur is quoted in *Saturday Evening Post*, October
24, 1942, p. 108.

[12] Eric McLoughlin, "Russian Children Taught in Defense," *New
York Times*, January 7, 1942, sec. 1, p. 6; Maurice Hindus, "The Russian Slogan: Work, Study, and Learn," *Reader's Digest* 44 (February
1944): 59–60.

[13] Irina Skariatina, "Victory at Rzhev," *Collier's*, January 23, 1943,
pp. 38–39.

[14] Rolf Singer, "Roaming Russia's Caucasus," *National Geographic
Magazine* 82 (July 1942): 91–121; Owen Lattimore, "New Road to

Writers frequently made sweeping comparisons of the people of the USSR and the man on the street of the United States. Both nations were said to be alike in their ethnic diversity, innate friendliness, even their mechanical ingenuity.[15] Were Yanks famous as back-slapping joiners? "Attend any dinner or lunch with the Russians," one correspondent wrote, "and you might just be at any Rotary Club luncheon in the United States of America."[16] Another claimed a typical general of the Red Army "reminds you of a good YMCA secretary."[17] The mode of living of our new allies was cast in American metaphors. Infantrymen from the Russian steppes became dogfaces from the Soviet great plains. Children's paramilitary groups were equated with the Boy Scouts.[18] The Volga was described as Russia's "Ol' Man River" whose famous boatmen really knew how to "tote dat barge."[19]

Such an approach emphasized an important distinction in the American attitude toward the USSR. The Russian citizenry was considered separate from the government above it. The soldier and the decent masses from which he came might be hailed enthusiastically because they supposedly bore no responsibility for the autocratic system and abhorrent policies imposed upon them. The *Saturday Evening Post* thus could deplore Soviet domestic tyranny and the economics of "collectivism and commissars" yet

Asia and Sunny Siberia," *National Geographic Magazine* 86 (December 1944): 641–676.

[15] Nila Magidoff, "Americans and Russians Are *So* Alike," *American Magazine* 138 (December 1944): 17, 118–120.

[16] Leland Stone, "Living with the Russians," *Rotarian* 62 (May 1943): 11.

[17] Quoted in Paul Willen, "Who 'Collaborated' with Russia?" *Antioch Review* 14 (September 1954): 264.

[18] Quentin Reynolds, "Children of Mars," *Collier's*, June 26, 1943, p. 11.

[19] Maynard Owen Williams, "Mother Volga Defends Her Own," *National Geographic Magazine* 82 (December 1942): 793.

still recognize an incalculable debt to the Russian people. Many other journalists concurred.[20]

Viewed from this angle, Stalin's regime was only an unfortunate historical growth, a wart on the otherwise admirable nose of Mother Russia. Yet there it was, a government many had condemned as vicious beyond parallel, and the American people had to learn to live with it. During the months after the German invasion of Russia, observers began to remark that the USSR was molting its more unattractive characteristics for a look more fitting to Western eyes. Always, for example, critics had portrayed the Soviet Union as the prime promoter of global atheism. Now, however, Stalin was said to be moving toward religious toleration. By the end of 1942, several articles noted promising changes: swelling church attendance, government printing of the Bible, and the official disbanding of the Society of the Militant Godless.[21] When the Russian Orthodox church received formal recognition by the Kremlin late in 1943, *Time* magazine devoted a cover story to the new lenience toward religion.[22] In the wake of such developments, even the conservative *Dallas Morning News* told its readers that, "since the basic Communistic concept is not anti-Christian," official discouragement of worship was rapidly coming to an end.[23]

Indeed, Soviet officials sometimes seemed ready to permit not just the privilege to praise God in public but also other rights essential to our concept of democracy. The executive director of the Associated Press noticed signs that augured for greater freedom of expression among the journalists of the USSR. That nation's constitution, in fact, guaranteed (on paper, at least) a

[20] *Saturday Evening Post*, June 19, 1943, p. 108.

[21] Irina Skariatina, "Vespers in Moscow," *Collier's*, January 2, 1943, pp. 17–18; *Time*, June 15, 1942, p. 40.

[22] *Time*, December 27, 1943, pp. 49–58.

[23] *Dallas Morning News*, February 4, 1942, sec. 2, p. 4; February 26, 1942, sec. 2, p. 2.

wide range of human rights, and some observers predicted those promises would be fulfilled once the emergency of war had passed.[24]

Others applied cosmetics to well-known blemishes on the Soviet past. Those persons condemned in the purge trials of the thirties, the public read, were not innocent victims of Stalin's paranoia, but German infiltrators laying the groundwork for Hitler's assault.[25] No longer was the Soviet Union described as the land where bourgeois morality had given way to free love and quickie divorces. Now the government fined those who were too casual in their relationships, encouraged stable family life, and subsidized the adoption of war orphans.[26] Accounts of Russian life accentuated and applauded positive social achievements since the revolution. The massive program for public education that had reduced drastically the illiteracy of czarist days, for instance, appealed to an American public dedicated to the ideal of free schooling for all.[27] Such treatment softened the older vision of a totalitarian state ruling a nation of slaves. Thus transformed, the Soviet ally might rest easier on the conscience of the resident of Peoria or Waxahachie.

Nor did the press stop with this more palatable view of Soviet social policy. The economic philosophy of the USSR drew equal attention. As the major world-wide competitor to capitalism, communism proved a troublesome element in the Allied com-

[24] An editorial in *Collier's*, December 18, 1943, p. 86, claimed that the Soviet government was "evolving from a sort of Fascism toward, apparently, something resembling our own and Great Britain's democracy." See also Alexander Werth, "Russia behind the Lines," *Nation*, April 18, 1942, pp. 454–456; Arthur Upham Pope, "Can Stalin's Russia Go Democratic?—Yes," *American Mercury* 58 (February 1944): 135–142; *Indianapolis News*, November 18, 1944, p. 6.

[25] *Atlanta Constitution*, January 5, 1942, p. 4.

[26] *Christian Century*, July 19, 1944, p. 844.

[27] *Newsweek*, May 17, 1943, pp. 76–78; *School and Society*, May 8, 1943, p. 536.

bination. But the American businessman could find some evidence that Russian leaders were finally coming to their senses. Small, independent businesses were tolerated as long as the owner could supply his own goods and labor. Peasants also might till small plots of their own and sell the produce for profits. Soviet planners reportedly were turning to wage incentives to inspire greater efforts from workers, and the most ambitious Horatio Algers in Russian industry could become well-paid executives who lived comfortably and even rode to work in chauffeured limousines.[28] All this smacked of private enterprise, and *Collier's* thought that communism had "faded out in the Russia of Josef Stalin."[29] In its place there appeared to be a benign mutation—"state capitalism," one writer called it, or "a capitalist state in a socialist framework."[30] Vague terms, certainly, but such lack of clarity permitted the public to live with an economic system long portrayed as its natural antagonist.

Alone, however, this more sanguine view of Russian internal affairs was not enough to calm the public's uneasiness. Crouching within many Americans was also the fear of a Soviet Union bent on expanding its influence into neighboring lands and eventually over the world. The 1939 alliance with German aggression conjured up the old spectre of a Bolshevik state spreading revolution through force of arms and manipulating agents who wormed their malignant way into capitalist countries. Yet this image, too, was to change. After Pearl Harbor, writers in the *New York Times* explained the nonaggression pact as Stalin's stalling game. Once Britain and France abandoned collective security at Munich, the argument ran, the Soviet leader

[28] Walter Duranty, "How Red Is Russia?" *Collier's*, February 28, 1942, pp. 20, 38–40; John Hersey, "Soviet Business Executive," *Life*, January 15, 1945, pp. 39–44.

[29] *Collier's*, April 3, 1943, p. 86.

[30] Ibid.; Duranty, "How Red Is Russia?" p. 40.

could only sidle up to Hitler to buy time in preparation for the German invasion that he knew was inevitable. Likewise, the attacks on Poland and Finland were interpreted as defensive maneuvers to pad Russia's western borders against the coming Nazi onslaught.[31] In the eyes of many, Stalin the brutal aggressor thus became Stalin the far-seeing realist who, as Albert Einstein told a New York audience, had pursued international security in the "most honest and unequivocal way."[32]

Such a verdict rested upon the belief that Soviet diplomats no longer shaped their policy according to Marxist principles but by the traditional desires of Russian nationalism. This change in purpose was traced back to the downfall and exile of Leon Trotsky in 1929. Once Stalin had triumphed over his rival, he supposedly had forsaken Trotsky's promotion of revolution for a more conservative course. The war had accelerated this transition and made it complete. Communist leaders, the public read, could never persuade the masses to lay down their lives to expand bolshevism. Only an appeal to the Soviet people's deep love of motherland could inspire the total dedication needed for victory.[33] Many writers predicted, moreover, that after the war Moscow would be too busy rebuilding and raising the standard of living to consider stretching its borders outward.[34]

The foremost advocate of this approach was Joseph Davies, ambassador to the Soviet Union from 1937 to 1938. In his bestselling *Mission to Moscow* and in many articles and published interviews, he portrayed Russian leaders as realistic men of good

---

[31] *Saint Louis Post-Dispatch*, August 18, 1941, sec. C, p. 2; Charles A. Merrill, "U.S. Must Accept Russia's New Role," *Boston Globe*, March 19, 1944, p. 4.

[32] *New York Times*, October 26, 1942, p. 17.

[33] *Dallas Morning News*, October 23, 1945, sec. 2, p. 2; *San Francisco Chronicle*, April 2, 1943, p. 14.

[34] John K. Jessup, "America and the Future," *Life*, September 20, 1943, pp. 109–110.

will who would continue to pursue a moderate and predictable
course in foreign affairs.[35] Indeed, all signs in Russia seemed
to point to a replacement of revolutionary zeal by a sensible,
cooperative policy. When the government scrapped the "Inter-
nationale," the call to arms to the world's working masses, and
substituted a more nationalistic anthem, the *New York Times*
solemnly praised the new melody and commended its composer
as a moderate who stood between the musical right and left.[36]

The dissolution of the Third Communist International, or
Comintern, in May 1943 removed the last lingering doubts of
many Americans. As the central director of communist parties in
other nations, the Comintern was singled out by Axis propa-
gandists and by critics of the USSR as evidence that Stalin's talk
of Allied unity was only so much twaddle. The official death of
the International, therefore, soothed that nagging fear. One by
one, America's big city dailies hailed the dissolution. "This action removes any real fear that Stalin will try to impose Russia's
form of government on other countries after the war," wrote
one conservative editor.[37] Others applauded the decision as "momentous" and "the smartest political move of the conflict."[38]

The hosannas given to Stalin for the death of the Comintern
indicated how drastically the image of the Soviet Union had
changed by mid-1943. It was left to *Life* magazine to give the
clearest expression to this new-found amity. That periodical's
entire issue of March 29, 1943, was given over to a broad-

[35] Joseph E. Davies, *Mission to Moscow*. For other expressions of Da-
vies' views, see "Is Communism a Menace to Us?" *New York Times
Magazine*, April 12, 1942, pp. 3, 36; "Russia Will Hold This Summer,"
Saturday Evening Post, June 20, 1942, pp. 16–17, 88–89; "What We
Didn't Know about Russia," *Reader's Digest* 40 (March 1942): 45–52.

[36] *New York Times*, January 4, 1944, sec. 1, p. 16.

[37] *Dallas Morning News*, May 24, 1943, sec. 2, p. 4.

[38] *New York Herald Tribune*, May 23, 1943, sec. 2, p. 6; *Denver Post*,
May 23, 1943, p. 2; *Saint Louis Post-Dispatch*, May 23, 1943, sec. D, p.
2; *San Francisco Chronicle*, May 24, 1943, p. 10.

ranging look at Russian society. *Life* editors described the Russians as "one hell of a people" who looked, dressed, and thought like Americans. Bustling cities, eager school children, humming industries, and manicured collective farms—all these testified to a nation striving toward modernity. Readers were told that the Russian secret police, the NKVD, was a national police force similar to the FBI. The outlook for postwar diplomacy was equally optimistic. In an extensive interview printed in the issue, Joseph Davies dismissed the fear of Soviet promotion of communism as "the same old red herring drawn across the trail." Although Stalin might demand some land along his western borders for security, he continued, Russian policy would be motivated "solely by humanitarian considerations." To be sure, the editors admitted that Soviet rulers had their shortcomings, but any doubts were overshadowed by the accomplishments wrought since the revolution. From first to last, the *Life* issue hammered home one idea to its readers: the USSR was mending its erring ways, and like a repentant ex-con it should be welcomed with compassion and trust into the society of civilized nations.[39]

To the millions who read such accounts in America's most popular magazines and newspapers, a remarkable metamorphosis seemed to have transformed Russia into a nation they could embrace with confidence. But a closer look would reveal a darker undercurrent of opinion in the country's press. Some editors never shared in the admiration of the new Russia. To these writers, the Soviet citizen lived under a tyranny as heinous as that of Nazi Germany. Nor did they believe Stalin had abandoned his dream of conquest. The Russian leader's policy of friendship, they argued, was only a new phase of an old campaign to overrun Europe and to inoculate capitalist societies with the virus of bolshevism. As usual, Americans sang

[39] *Life*, March 29, 1943. For Davies interview, see pp. 49–55.

not in unison but with many voices. Behind the hymns of praise for our new ally could be heard dirges warning that Soviet smiles hid a danger to our civilization as great as ever before. These fears formed another, less recognized theme in the wartime press.

The religious press, which often had distrusted Soviet intentions in the past, continued to harbor some doubts about the Russian bear throughout the war. Some sources, such as the Baptist *Watchman-Examiner*, cheered the apparent Soviet relaxation of church restrictions, but the image of a Godless Russia did not die easily.[40] To the *Christian Century*, religious leaders had been puppets of the czars, and now they would dance to the commands of an atheist dictator.[41] Of all denominations, the Roman Catholic press leveled the most vigorous sustained attacks upon the Soviet Union. The Church of Rome counted millions of followers in the lands of eastern and southern Europe that lay before the advancing Red Army. Church periodicals, reflecting a fear for the future of these groups among American Catholics, issued some of the most vitriolic anti-Russian rhetoric of the war. The moderate Jesuit weekly, *America*, expressed guarded hope over the growth of nationalism in Russia, yet its editors scoffed at Stalin's new lenience toward religion as a program of meaningless half-reforms.[42] Such hostility, however, paled beside that of another church periodical, *The Catholic World*. Month after month, that journal's editor, James M. Gillis, railed against Russia and its American sympathizers. Any talk of future friendship with the USSR he dismissed as "so much crooked thinking, loose logic and propa-

[40] *Watchman-Examiner* (New York), May 2, 1942, pp. 527–528.

[41] *Christian Century*, September 15, 1943, p. 1029; September 27, 1944, pp. 1103–1104.

[42] *America*, October 31, 1942, pp. 99–100; February 27, 1943, pp. 537–538; June 4, 1943, p. 238.

gandistic blah-blah."[43] Hitler and Stalin, he wrote, were no more different than Pilate and Herod; both sought to smother the love of God through the absolute control of the state.[44] By portraying Germany and Russia as totalitarian kinsmen, Gillis thus considered World War II as merely a prologue to the real showdown after the defeat of the Axis. "The reconstruction of the world," he predicted, "will be either on a Communistic or a Democratic basis. One or the other. They cannot be combined."[45]

Spokesmen for the business community, as vigorous defenders of capitalism, viewed our rapprochement with Soviet Russia with mixed emotions. "You can do business with Stalin!" promised Raymond Moley in *Newsweek*, and other economic analysts predicted that Soviet trade would contribute to American prosperity.[46] Already U.S. industry was sending Russia everything from locomotives to canned stew to aid in the struggle against Germany. After the war, American business might supply the consumer goods demanded by the sacrificing citizens of the USSR, while our machines, engineers, and technicians might help raise their standard of living. In exchange, our new partners could export the furs, timber, gold, manganese, platinum, and chromium needed by our economy.[47] Upon his return from a tour of the Soviet Union, Eric Johnston, president of the U.S. Chamber of Commerce, spoke confidently of the profits waiting for American businessmen in what another writer called *"the largest single market ever known!"*[48] Thus the bogey of

[43] *Catholic World* 155 (August 1942): 513.

[44] *Catholic World* 155 (June 1942): 261–265.

[45] Ibid., p. 262.

[46] Raymond Moley, "You Can Do Business with Stalin," *Newsweek*, October 18, 1943, p. 112.

[47] *Business Week*, June 20, 1942, p. 80; *U.S. News and World Report*, December 3, 1943, pp. 20–21; *Fortune* 31 (January 1945): 153–156.

[48] Eric Johnston, "Russian Visit," *Life*, September 11, 1944, pp. 100–

the postwar depression might be dispelled if a booming trade
were struck up with Soviet Russia.

It was an attractive vision of mutual economic backscratching.
But what if Russia didn't have the itch? Some business commentators foresaw not cooperation but competition between the
United States and the Soviet Union. In the wake of the war's
destruction, reasoned a writer for *U.S. News and World Report*,
the developing nations of Europe and the Third World would
search for the economic system best designed to deliver the
goods and jobs for peacetime prosperity. By guaranteeing full
employment and exploiting resources, communist planners could
give the illusion of explosive progress and thereby win the admiration—and the political allegiance—of the planet's under-
privileged peoples.[49]

Occasionally writers in the business press elevated this difference in economic systems to an irrepressible struggle between
two ways of life. The *Wall Street Journal* columnist Thomas
Woodlock provides an instructive example. He reasoned that
state control of the economy violated certain basic human desires; thus a leader such as Stalin had to suppress all liberties
of his subjects in order to stay in power. Once free of popular
restraints, furthermore, a totalitarian ruler would turn invariably
to aggression against his neighbors. The procession from economic concentration to military adventure would unfold naturally in Russia as it had in Germany and Japan.[50] Like Father
Gillis, such journalists placed the USSR with our enemies in
the same category of "totalitarian states." And, not surprisingly,
they came to the same conclusion: Even after the surrender of

116; Harland H. Allen, "Looking Ahead with Russia," *Rotarian* 64
(February 1944): 25–26.

[49] *U.S. News and World Report*, September 3, 1943, pp. 13–14.

[50] *Wall Street Journal*, February 4, 1942, p. 6; June 2, 1943, p. 4;
January 21, 1944, p. 4; August 2, 1944, p. 4.

the Axis powers, world diplomacy would remain dangerously unstable as long as the Soviet form of government survived. "There can be no assurance of peace," wrote David Lawrence of *U.S. News*, "until Russia becomes a free nation."[51]

Elsewhere a group of respected intellectuals were criticizing what they considered almost a deification of Russia and its leaders. Among others, Eugene Lyons, William Henry Chamberlin, and Max Eastman, all of whom had sympathized with the Soviet experiment in the past, warned against the "mush-heads" who were deluding the public with "piffle" about a reformed Russia.[52] As editor of *American Mercury*, Lyons reminded his readers of Stalin's cynical control of public opinion and suppression of all dissent.[53] The others wrote of a society denied the freedoms of speech and religion and suffering under a legal system based not on the right of *habeas corpus* but of *habeas cadaver*.[54] To all three, any government faced as its first duty the protection of civil liberties. All the accomplishments of the Kremlin could not compensate for its violation of what Chamberlin called "the inalienable right of the human personality."[55]

This harsher image of Russian life was not confined to these critics and to the religious and business press. Thumbing

[51] David Lawrence, "When Will Russia Become a 'Free' Nation?" *U.S. News and World Report*, October 29, 1943, pp. 32–33.

[52] Max Eastman, "We Must Face Facts about Russia," *Reader's Digest* 43 (July 1943): 1–14; Eugene Lyons, "The Library: Soviet Foreign Policies," *American Mercury* 56 (March 1943): 367–373.

[53] For examples of Lyons' views, see "The Library: Soviet Foreign Policies"; "The State of the Union: An Open Letter to Vice-President Wallace," *American Mercury* 56 (January 1943): 31–37; "The Library: The Purification of Stalin," *American Mercury* 54 (January 1942): 109–116.

[54] William Henry Chamberlin, "Can Stalin's Russia Go Democratic? —No," *American Mercury* 58 (February 1944): 142–148.

[55] William Henry Chamberlin, "Clinical Notes: The Liberal Label," *American Mercury* 57 (October 1943): 467–468.

through the pages of the country's big city dailies, American readers could find many of the same misgivings. A few newspapers stood apart from the rest. The bitterest critics of the New Deal's domestic and foreign policies, for example, did not declare a total moratorium during the emergency of global war. In particular, Colonel Robert McCormick's *Chicago Tribune* and *Washington Times-Herald* and the chain of papers owned by William Randolph Hearst, of which the *New York Journal-American* and *San Francisco Examiner* were the most prominent, counseled that contact with the USSR could only do mischief to our fundamental institutions. A pair of headlines taken from their pages suggested the drift of many articles in these journals: "Red Wave Threatens to Drown Christian Civilization" and "Soviet Union Is Only Aggressor in the World."[56] Yet other representatives of the press closer to the American mainstream also questioned the wisdom of friendlier U.S.-Soviet relations, and virtually every major newspaper expressed some uneasiness over Russia's treatment of its neighbors abroad and its people at home.

On one point, at least, many editors could agree: friendship with the Soviet Union did not include acceptance of communists on the home front. As usual, the McCormick-Hearst press issued the shrillest warnings against radicalism. To these journalists no part of American life was immune to communist influence. The relationship between President Roosevelt and American communists, the *Tribune* assured its readers, was "one of the utmost intimacy," and the chief executive was packing the government bureaucracy with men of dangerous ideas.[57] From Hol-

[56] These headlines are quoted in Thomas A. Bailey, *America Faces Russia: Russian-American Relations from Early Times to Our Day*, p. 298.

[57] *Chicago Tribune*, January 31, 1944, p. 10. The *San Francisco Examiner*, December 24, 1941, p. 6, believed J. Edgar Hoover to be the main target of communists in the government.

lywood came "A LONG SUCCESSION OF INSIDIOUS AND EVIL
MOTION PICTURES," which undermined respect for our national
heritage.[58] When a national survey revealed an appalling ignorance of U.S. history among public school children, the
Journal-American blamed not incompetent teachers or dull students but "a gigantic LEFT-WING CONSPIRACY" designed to
snuff out youthful patriotism.[59]

Other journals may not have seen Bolsheviks under every
bed and school desk, but they often admitted more than a grain
of truth in such charges. Some never believed that the dissolution of the Communist International spelled the end of all
promotion of revolution. Despite the death of the Comintern,
the arch-Republican *Philadelphia Inquirer* warned Americans
not to let down their guard against the "treacherous chiseling of
Red Agents," and the *Los Angeles Times* also advised a wait-
and-see attitude.[60] To protect against internal subversion, such
editors called for special attention to radical infiltration of labor
unions.[61] At the very least, "notorious pinks" and fellow travel-
ers should be cut from the federal payroll, and a few writers
recommended deportation of communist aliens and the curtail-
ment of political activities of the Communist Party of America.[62]

While these journalists were claiming that Soviet leaders
might still be stirring revolution in our midst, others were em-
phasizing the more distressing side of Soviet society. In April
1943 word leaked to the West that two moderate Polish labor
leaders, Henryk Ehrlick and Victor Alter, had been executed for
war crimes in the USSR, apparently without benefit of trial. As
union officials and Polish-Americans rallied in protest, persistent

[58] *New York Journal-American*, February 10, 1944, p. 14.
[59] Ibid., April 20, 1943, p. 18.
[60] *Philadelphia Inquirer*, May 24, 1943, p. 10; *Los Angeles Times*,
May 23, 1943, sec. 2, p. 4.
[61] *Denver Post*, May 27, 1943, p. 2.
[62] *Los Angeles Times*, January 17, 1942, p. 4; May 27, 1943, p. 4.

critics of Stalin clucked their collective tongues, and more sympathetic papers, like the *San Francisco Chronicle*, could only comment lamely that there was no proof the dead men were innocent.[63] Near the end of 1944, reporter William L. White published in *Reader's Digest* his "Report on the Russians," which challenged the claim that the Revolution of 1917 had brought economic security to the Soviet worker. On his visit to the USSR, White found that the average factory reminded him of a "moderately well-run penitentiary" whose inhabitants lived in poverty more abject than that of depression America. Instead of an equal division of wealth, White found that factory managers ate caviar and monopolized the automobiles, while the working stiff could not afford toilet paper. And for all this, bureaucratic control and the lack of competition left Russian industry hopelessly inefficient.[64] Almost as tragic to other writers was the withering of Russia's rich cultural life under the stifling control of the state; instead of the novels of a Tolstoy or the symphonies of a Tchaikovsky, artists were forced to churn out folk themes and hymns to hydroelectric plants.[65] Taken together, such varied observations painted a portrait of the worst of all possible worlds: slavery and starvation, want unrelieved by any sense of individual dignity.

Disturbing enough, such images of Soviet domestic tyranny, but more alarming were the claims of some journalists that Stalin had no intention of continuing to act in concert with Western diplomats once the Axis was defeated. Uneasiness about the future foreign policy of the USSR seldom was voiced openly. The vague, optimistic statements issued after wartime

[63] *Christian Century*, April 21, 1943, pp. 475–476; *San Francisco Chronicle*, April 1, 1943, p. 14.

[64] William L. White, "Report on the Russians," *Reader's Digest* 45 (December 1944): 115–122.

[65] Nicolas Nabokov, "Music under Dictatorship," *Atlantic Monthly* 169 (January 1942): 92–99.

conferences of Allied leaders usually passed over disagreements and implied that postwar cooperation would come with a minimum of strain. In retrospect, however, many editors seem to have been less confident that all would go so smoothly.

A tiny minority of writers suspected that Stalin might desert the U.S. and Britain for a new alliance with Hitler, while the Hearst press speculated that Russia would align itself closely with Japan against the Allies because of the common Asiatic nature of both peoples. The *Journal-American* even provided photographs of Soviet generals with Mongoloid features as proof of this bizarre theory of Oriental solidarity.[66]

More often uneasiness surfaced in the wake of odd, almost forgotten events of those years. In January 1944, for example, the official Soviet newspaper *Pravda* published two apparently unrelated articles—one charging that Great Britain was negotiating a unilateral peace with Germany, the other bitterly attacking the Republican politician Wendell Willkie, known for his conciliatory approach to Soviet diplomacy.[67] Amid the astounding outpouring of opinion that followed, several voices warned that Stalin was beginning to cool relations with the West in preparation for a more independent, hostile policy once victory was assured.[68]

Such random episodes hinted that doubts of Russian sincerity lay closer to the surface than many would admit. The most important testing ground of cooperation was the rim of states along the western border of the USSR. On the surface, the American press appeared conciliatory over the future of this region. Most editors, for instance, accepted as reasonable the Soviet

[66] *New York Journal-American*, February 4, 1944, p. 14.

[67] *New York Times*, January 6, 1944, sec. 1, p. 1.

[68] *Wall Street Journal*, January 7, 1944, p. 6; *Dallas Morning News*, January 7, 1944, sec. 2, p. 2; *Los Angeles Times*, January 20, 1944, p. 4; *Denver Post*, January 6, 1944, p. 2; *Washington Post*, January 7, 1944, p. 9; *Philadelphia Inquirer*, January 19, 1944, p. 14.

desire to have friendly governments in Eastern Europe to discourage invasions of Russia like those that had wreaked havoc
twice in three decades.[69] Yet in one sense this concession was
dangerously ambiguous, for the crucial question was not
whether, but how, these buffer states were to be created. Stalin,
after all, had accepted the principle of self-determination expressed in the Declaration of the United Nations. When writers
agreed on the desirability of pro-Soviet regimes in Eastern Europe, therefore, they usually did so on the condition that such
governments would rest on the consent of the voters of those
nations.[70]

Evidence was mounting, however, that the Kremlin would allow something less than unhampered political development
along its western boundaries. By early 1944, Stalin had annexed
the Baltic states, Bessarabia, and part of Bucovina, and had announced that a section of eastern Poland would be added soon
after Russian occupation. The leftist exile groups in Moscow,
the Polish Lublin Committee and the Free German Committee,
seemed groomed to extend Soviet influence into European postwar politics, while the success of the communist-led guerillas in
Yugoslavia seemed to presage a growth of Russian power in that
region.

This turn of events eroded sharply the confidence in the
ability of the U.S. and Britain to work in harmony with the
Soviet Union after the war. All these actions had been carried

---

[69] *Atlanta Constitution*, January 29, 1944, p. 4; *Washington Post*,
April 6, 1943, p. 11.

[70] For example, editors who often wrote that Russia had earned a secure western border also emphasized Stalin's promise of a strong, independent Polish government founded on self-determination. See *New
York Herald Tribune*, April 7, 1943, p. 26; May 9, 1943, sec. 2, p. 8;
also *Saint Louis Post-Dispatch*, January 8, 1944, sec. A, p. 4; *San Francisco Chronicle*, May 7, 1943, p. 14.

out without consulting the Western powers, and at best such developments summoned up the old image of a secretive, suspicious Stalin rejecting collective security and ruling in isolation to the east.[71] At worst, Stalin's policy seemed to herald a new age of insecurity and fear, of aggression, revolution, and rightist reaction, for no European nation could rest safe, it was said, as long as one of their number failed to acknowledge the right of any people to life under a government of their own choosing.[72] "The American people," wrote the editors of the New York Times, "will not approve . . . a system which takes over from Axis ideology the scheme for dividing the world among the victors."[73] While most editors held out hope for cooperation and compromise, their doubts and speculations over Soviet intentions in Eastern Europe suggested they looked to the future with growing misgivings.

All this does not mean that spokesmen for the national press were uniformly unfriendly and distrustful of their Soviet ally. Rather it suggests that attitudes toward Russia were more divided and contradictory than we usually remember. Dominating the popular press was the image of a valiant Russian people ruled by a government rapidly abandoning its dictatorial ways. Yet the continuing reminders of Stalin's dictatorship and misgivings over the heavy Soviet hand in Eastern Europe tempered this admiration. During the two years following the end of the war in Europe, the mounting disagreements among the

[71] New York Herald Tribune, April 28, 1943, p. 26; Dallas Morning News, April 28, 1943, sec. 2, p. 2; Denver Post, April 27, 1943, p. 2; Washington Post, January 5, 1944, p. 8; Barnet Nover, "Russia and Poland," Washington Post, January 13, 1944, p. 9; Philadelphia Inquirer, January 13, 1944, p. 10.

[72] New York Times, April 26, 1943, sec. C, p. 18; Dallas Morning News, January 12, 1944, sec. 2, p. 2.

[73] New York Times, August 6, 1944, sec. E, p. 8.

Allies appeared to confirm the worst suspicions of Russia's critics, and the prevailing image of the USSR began to change again—this time for the worse.

To most Americans, the goals of the Second World War were supremely simple. Beyond the demand of unconditional surrender, our blood was spilled and our treasure spent to guarantee individual liberty, political self-expression, and a new organization to keep the peace in the community of nations. Stalin's acceptance of the principles of the Atlantic Charter and the outward accord of wartime conferences nurtured the belief that such a vision was entirely realistic.

But events soon proved how such a general blueprint could conceal bitter disputes among the Allies. The confidence, such as that following the Moscow Conference of 1943, was not to be fulfilled, for the Council of Foreign Ministers deadlocked in the composing of treaties with the defeated Axis powers in the fall of 1945, and Russia proceeded to impose pro-Soviet governments in the Eastern European lands it occupied. The temporary division of Germany looked more and more permanent as the victors failed to agree how to punish their common enemy. In the Far East, the USSR appeared to expand its influence into Korea, Manchuria, and Mongolia as civil war smoldered in China. Early in 1946, Soviet demands on Iran and Turkey and the struggle of communist insurgents in Greece seemed to signal an assault on the eastern Mediterranean first to outflank and then to overrun the countries of Western Europe.

In the wake of these developments, the elements of Russia's unattractive image began to re-emerge. There was not yet the widespread, near-hysterical fear of an expansionist communism that would come with the McCarthy era. But more and more often Americans read of a secretive Soviet Union whose aggressive designs on neighboring nations threatened to upset the newborn peace. The speed with which this more hostile view appeared is indicated by the editorial reception to Winston Churchill's "iron curtain" address delivered in Fulton, Missouri, in March 1946. Most editors roundly rejected Churchill's suggestion of a military alliance of Britain and the United States and preferred to rely on the machinery of the United Nations for resolving any disputes. Yet many also accepted the former prime minister's analysis of a regime in Moscow extending totalitarianism over Eastern Europe and threatening the security of the Western powers.[74]

Just as important as this suspicion itself was the context in which the Russian threat was perceived. During the final years of war and the months that followed, some writers drew comparisons between the policies and techniques of expansion of the USSR and those of the recently defeated Axis nations, especially Germany. Communists in Western Europe and the United States were dubbed the new fifth column of Bolshevik Quislings.[75] To the *Saint Louis Post-Dispatch*, elections held under the guns of the Red Army were echoes of the sham plebiscites in the wake of earlier German advances.[76] The stockpiling of such strategic materials as tungsten was compared ominously with similar programs under Hitler before the war.[77] Writers even pointed to the use of the goose step by Soviet troops as an indication that militarism was running rampant in Russia as it

[74] *San Francisco Chronicle*, March 7, 1946, p. 14; *Los Angeles Times*, March 7, 1946, p. 4; *Atlanta Constitution*, March 4, 1946, p. 6; *Philadelphia Inquirer*, March 6, 1946, p. 20; and *Phoenix Republic*, March 1, 1946, p. 10; March 8, 1946, p. 10. For example, the *Salt Lake Tribune*, often sympathetic with the Soviet Union, opposed a British alliance but added, "To almost every other sentiment expressed there will be agreement" (March 7, 1946, p. 8).

[75] J. Edgar Hoover, "Red Fascism in the United States Today," *American Magazine* 143 (February 1947): 24–25, 87–90; *Watchman-Examiner* (New York), September 5, 1946, p. 915.

[76] *Saint Louis Post-Dispatch*, October 24, 1945, sec. C, p. 2.

[77] *Iron Age*, June 26, 1947, p. 98.

had in Germany.[78] When commentators did distinguish between the Russian and Nazi experiences, the differences they
saw often were virtually meaningless. To the *Los Angeles Times*
political editor, a follower of the Soviet line was only more
dangerous than the devotee of national socialism. "Your Fascist," he explained, "is dumb, [while] your Communist . . . is
sly, slick and resourceful."[79] Such writers paid little attention to
the philosophical distinctions between communism and national
socialism. More important, they all but ignored differences in
the historical experiences and drives of Germany and Russia.
Accepted literally, such comparisons of the USSR and Germany
taught that Stalin was applying Hitlerian techniques to build a
Soviet Reich upon the ruins of Europe and eventually over the
world. From this point of view, the sources of conduct, and
therefore the threats, of both nations were the same. As one
columnist warned his readers, "The pattern that Russia has laid
down is precisely the Hitler pattern in the years before the
World War."[80]

The lesson was obvious: if prewar leaders had failed to stand
up to Hitler until it was too late, now Stalin had to be stopped
before he wrapped the world again in flames. In a final parallel
with wartime, America was said to stand at a new Munich.[81]
The time had come to halt the advance of Red fascism. Those
who still called for a compromise with Soviet power risked

[78] Adler and Patterson, "Red Fascism," pp. 1051–1064. See also Paul
Mallon, "The Churchill-Stalin Debate," *Seattle Post-Intelligencer*, March
26, 1946, p. 8; David Lawrence, "Russ Imperialism Likened to Hitler,
Czarist Regimes," *Salt Lake Tribune*, March 23, 1946, p. 4.

[79] *Los Angeles Times*, March 24, 1946, p. 4.

[80] John Perry Wood, "Mr. Truman 'Not Alarmed,'" *Los Angeles
Times*, March 17, 1946, p. 4.

[81] Joseph Alsop, "On the Eve of Crisis," *Los Angeles Times*, March
16, 1946, p. 4.

being condemned as modern-day Chamberlins trying to appease the unappeaseable.[82]

In this climate of opinion, the press responded enthusiastically to the presidential statement of the Truman Doctrine in March 1947. By asking for $400 million in aid to Greece and Turkey, President Harry Truman seemed to be standing steadfast against a policy of appeasement. But more than that, he reduced all diplomacy to a struggle between the forces of freedom and oppression, and he identified the Soviet danger with the totalitarianism of Germany and Japan. Thus the president bestowed official blessings on those critics who perceived our nation standing toe to toe with Russia in a new phase of the same struggle that had seen the Axis go down to defeat. The Truman Doctrine crystallized and sharpened the hostile image of the Soviet Union and brought full circle the development of attitudes since the United States had joined its strength with Russia six years earlier.

The Truman Doctrine was as close as this country would come to a formal declaration of the cold war. As such it offers a vantage point from which to look back over the images of the Soviet Union as reflected in the American press. During World War II, the vast majority of outlets of popular opinion usually claimed that the Soviet government was adopting policies that rested easy on the public mind. The Russian people, often portrayed almost as borsht-eating Americans, supposedly were enjoying at last those freedoms denied them under the czars and the prewar leadership of the Kremlin, while Stalin and his diplomatic corps reportedly had embraced the principle of collective security. The future seemed to promise an era of peace

[82] William Henry Chamberlin, "Appeasement Is Bankrupt," *Seattle Post-Intelligencer*, March 18, 1946, p. 10; *Saturday Evening Post*, October 12, 1946, p. 160.

within a world community united by mutual trust and liberal
democratic ideals.

Yet suspicions of the USSR never died during the years of
war, and in fact remained stronger than usually is recalled.
Uneasiness over continuing reminders of Soviet dictatorship was
matched by mounting evidence that Stalin intended to bring
Eastern Europe under his hegemony and was not overly concerned with the niceties of the electoral process. These fore-
bodings appeared most often in the church and business press,
in the McCormick and Hearst journals, and in conservative Republican newspapers. But virtually all sources regarded Russia
with some disenchantment during the war's final two years.

These conflicting images suggest an ambivalence in the public's mind, which made the outward friendship toward Soviet
Russia more unstable than it appeared.[83] After 1945, when it
became clear the USSR did not fit the optimistic image dominant during wartime, editors fell back upon the only other
alternative available, and the view of a villainous and bullying
Russia quickly took over. Comparisons between the Soviet
Union and Nazi Germany only accelerated this change.

How does all this add to our understanding of the origins of
the cold war? This description of the currents of popular opinion
tells us nothing, of course, about the motives of national leaders—whether President Truman, for example, acted as an aggressor or a defender of Western civilization. Such a study,
however, does tend to confirm the conclusion of such historians
as Louis Halle who avoid the assessment of guilt and stress

[83] One contemporary student of popular opinion wrote in 1943, "Certainly as far as the Russians are concerned, one cannot conclude that
our common military course has induced a feeling of friendship and
willingness to cooperate fully with them." His observation was based
on a study of opinion polls taken during the first two years of war (Ross
Stagner, "Public Opinion and Peace Plans," *Public Opinion Quarterly*
7 [Summer 1943]: 301).

instead the virtual inevitability of the cold war.[84] At the level of popular perception that formed the underpinnings of official decision making, a drastic reaction in the public's views of the USSR would have been difficult to avoid, for World War II ended with the American people ripe for disillusionment with their Soviet ally.

The war thrust upon this country responsibilities it no longer could ignore. The collapse of Hitler's Reich left the continent close to chaos and created a power vacuum in east and central Europe. Into this region marched the armies of a nation of which our people knew little and understood less. It was an immensely complex diplomatic situation that required sophistication and patience. To cope with these circumstances, however, the war bequeathed to the public two extreme views of Russia— one naively predicting an era of unblemished peace, the other warning of a brutal, revolutionary system unalterably opposed to our values. Russia "appears to us either as god, devil, or another America," wrote the editors of *Life* magazine.[85] The harsh realities of the postwar world inevitably shattered the first optimistic image, and with its passing the old hostility ruled again as it had until late 1941. The war thus raised our hopes impossibly high and left us with only a terrifying vision when those hopes were dashed. And, finally, the world war, by definition, encouraged everyone to think of diplomacy in sweeping, global terms, and it strengthened what might be called an "Armageddon outlook." In 1945 the Allies had just defeated a world-wide Axis coalition; to many, nothing seemed more natural than to consider the mounting disagreements with Soviet leaders as the opening shots of a new struggle for control of the planet between the forces of wickedness and the legion of the good.

[84] Louis J. Halle, *The Cold War As History.*
[85] *Life,* July 17, 1944, p. 26.

From the perspective of a quarter-century, the swift collapse of popular confidence and friendship seems understandable, even unavoidable. As Americans looked eastward across Europe, they beheld the Russians, as Max Lerner wrote, with "the mingled fear and awe with which a Roman patrician regarded the barbarian tribes."[86] As the Soviet Union fell heir to the popular hatreds whipped up during the struggle against Germany and Japan, no charge against our former ally in arms was too grotesque to be believed. Witness, for instance, the testimony of William Bullitt, former ambassador to the Soviet Union, before Rep. John E. Rankin, chairman of the House Committee on Un-American Activities in 1946:

Rankin: Is it true that they eat human bodies in Russia?
Bullitt: I did see a picture of a skeleton of a child eaten by its parents.
Rankin: Then they're just human slaves in Russia?
Bullitt: There are more human slaves in Russia than ever existed anywhere in the world.[87]

When claims of slavery, infanticide, and cannibalism were featured in the national press, Americans saw a face of Russia far different from that of several months earlier. In fact, the friendship of 1941–1945 seems in retrospect a briefly blooming oasis at once created and doomed by the same frantic atmosphere of a nation in crisis. Ironically, the four years that saw the closest U.S.-Soviet cooperation of the century laid the foundations for the era of their greatest hostility. The traumas of the next few years honed the Soviet image and helped create a climate of opinion congenial to the government's escalating antagonism toward the USSR. Out of the frustrated hopes and lingering dread of wartime, there grew among the American people a glacial anxiety that would be a long time thawing.

[86] Max Lerner, "Russia and the Future," *Atlantic Monthly* 170 (November 1942): 79.
[87] Quoted in James Aronson, *The Press and the Cold War*, p. 32.

BIBLIOGRAPHY

Adler, Les K., and Thomas G. Patterson. "Red Fascism: The Merger of Nazi Germany and Soviet Russia in the American Image of Totalitarianism, 1930's–1950's." *American Historical Review* 75 (April 1970): 1049–1064.

Allen, Harland H. "Looking Ahead with Russia." *Rotarian* 64 (February 1944): 25–26.

Alsop, Joseph. "On the Eve of Crisis." *Los Angeles Times*, March 16, 1946, p. 4.

Aronson, James. *The Press and the Cold War*. New York: Bobbs-Merrill Co., 1970.

Atlanta Constitution, 1940–1947.

Bailey, Thomas A. *America Faces Russia: Russian-American Relations from Early Times to Our Day*. Gloucester, Mass.: Peter Smith, 1964.

Boston Globe, 1943–1947.

Chamberlin, William Henry. "Appeasement Is Bankrupt." *Seattle Post-Intelligencer*, March 18, 1946, p. 10.

———. "Can Stalin's Russia Go Democratic?—No." *American Mercury* 58 (February 1944): 142–148.

———. "Clinical Notes: The Liberal Label." *American Mercury* 57 (October 1943): 467–468.

Chicago Tribune, 1941–1947.

Curie, Eve. "Reds Determined." *Dallas Morning News*, January 8, 1942, sec. 2, p. 3.

Dallas Morning News, 1941–1947.

Davies, Joseph E. "Is Communism a Menace to Us?" *New York Times Magazine*, April 12, 1942, pp. 3, 36.

———. *Mission to Moscow*. New York: Simon and Schuster, 1941.

———. "Russia Will Hold This Summer." *Saturday Evening Post*, June 20, 1942, pp. 16–17, 88–89.

————. "What We Didn't Know about Russia." *Reader's Digest* 40 (March 1942): 45–52.

Dawson, Raymond H. *The Decision to Aid Russia, 1941: Foreign and Domestic Politics.* Chapel Hill: University of North Carolina Press, 1959.

Denver Post, 1939–1947.

Dewey, Donald O. "America and Russia 1939–1941: The Views of the New York *Times.*" *Journalism Quarterly* 44 (Spring 1967): 62–70.

Duranty, Walter. "How Red Is Russia?" *Collier's*, February 28, 1942, pp. 20, 38–40.

Eastman, Max. "We Must Face Facts about Russia." *Reader's Digest* 43 (July 1943): 1–14.

Filene, Peter G. *Americans and the Soviet Experiment, 1917–1933.* Cambridge: Harvard University Press, 1967.

Graebner, Norman A. "Cold War Origins and the Contemporary Debate." *Journal of Conflict Resolution* 13 (March 1969): 123–132.

Halle, Louis J. *The Cold War As History.* New York: Harper and Row, 1967.

Hersey, John. "Soviet Business Executive." *Life*, January 15, 1945, pp. 39–44.

Hindus, Maurice. "The Russian Slogan: Work, Study, and Learn." *Reader's Digest* 44 (February 1944): 59–60.

Hoover, J. Edgar. "Red Fascism in the United States Today." *American Magazine* 143 (February 1947): 24–25, 87–90.

Indianapolis News, 1943–1944.

Jessup, John K. "America and the Future." *Life*, September 20, 1943, pp. 109–110.

Johnston, Eric. "Russian Visit." *Life*, September 11, 1944, pp. 100–116.

Lasch, Christopher. "The Cold War Revisited and Revisioned." *New York Times Magazine*, January 14, 1968, pp. 26–27, 44–59.

Lattimore, Owen. "New Road to Asia and Sunny Siberia." *National Geographic Magazine* 86 (December 1944): 641–676.

Lawrence, David. "Russ Imperialism Likened to Hitler, Czarist Regimes." *Salt Lake Tribune*, March 23, 1946, p. 4.

————. "When Will Russia Become a 'Free' Nation?" *U.S. News and World Report*, October 29, 1943, pp. 32–33.

Lerner, Max. "Russia and the Future." *Atlantic Monthly* 170 (November 1942): 79–87.

Los Angeles Times, 1941–1947.

Lyons, Eugene. "The Library: Soviet Foreign Policies." *American Mercury* 56 (March 1943): 367–373.

———. "The Library: The Purification of Stalin." *American Mercury* 54 (January 1942): 109–116.

———. "The State of the Union: An Open Letter to Vice-President Wallace." *American Mercury* 56 (January 1943): 31–37.

McLemore, Henry. "Brave Russia." *Dallas Morning News*, January 26, 1942, sec. 2, p. 3.

McLoughlin, Eric. "Russian Children Taught in Defense." *New York Times*, January 7, 1942, sec. 1, p. 6.

Magidoff, Nila. "Americans and Russians Are *So* Alike." *American Magazine* 138 (December 1944): 17, 118–120.

Merrill, Charles A. "U.S. Must Accept Russia's New Role." *Boston Globe*, March 19, 1944, p. 4.

Moley, Raymond. "You Can Do Business with Stalin." *Newsweek*, October 18, 1943, p. 112.

Nabokov, Nicolas. "Music under Dictatorship." *Atlantic Monthly* 169 (January 1942): 92–99.

New York Herald Tribune, 1939–1947.

New York Journal-American, 1941–1947.

New York Times, 1941–1947.

Nover, Barnet. "Russia and Poland." *Washington Post*, January 13, 1944, p. 9.

Pachter, Henry. "Revisionist Historians and the Cold War." *Dissent* 15 (November 1968): 505–518.

Philadelphia Inquirer, 1943–1947.

Phoenix Republic, 1946.

Pope, Arthur Upham. "Can Stalin's Russia Go Democratic?—Yes." *American Mercury* 58 (February 1944): 135–142.

Reynolds, Quentin. "Children of Mars." *Collier's*, June 26, 1943, p. 11.

Saint Louis Post-Dispatch, 1941–1947.

Salt Lake Tribune, 1946.

San Francisco Chronicle, 1941–1947.

San Francisco Examiner, 1941–1943.

Seabury, Paul. "Cold War Origins, I." *Journal of Contemporary History* 3 (January 1968): 169–182.

Seattle Post-Intelligencer, 1946.

Singer, Rolf. "Roaming Russia's Caucasus." *National Geographic Magazine* 82 (July 1942): 91–121.

Skariatina, Irina. "Vespers in Moscow." *Collier's*, January 2, 1943, pp. 17–18.

————. "Victory at Rzhev." *Collier's*, January 23, 1943, pp. 38–39.

Snell, John. "The Cold War: Four Contemporary Appraisals." *American Historical Review* 68 (October 1962): 69–75.

Sobel, Robert. *The Origins of Interventionism: The United States and the Russo-Finnish War*. New York: Bookman Associates, 1960.

Spanier, John W. *American Foreign Policy since World War II*. New York: Frederick A. Praeger, 1965.

Stagner, Ross. "Public Opinion and Peace Plans." *Public Opinion Quarterly* 7 (Summer 1943): 301.

Stone, Leland. "Living with the Russians." *Rotarian* 62 (May 1943): 11.

Sulzberger, C. L. "Sergei, Red Fighter." *New York Times Magazine*, January 4, 1942, pp. 4, 23.

Thomas, Brian. "Cold War Origins, II." *Journal of Contemporary History* 3 (January 1968): 183–198.

Wall Street Journal, 1941–1947.

Warren, Frank A., III. *Liberals and Communism: The "Red Decade" Revisited*. Bloomington: Indiana University Press, 1966.

Washington Post, 1941–1947.

Watchman-Examiner (New York), 1941–1947.

Werth, Alexander. "Russia behind the Lines." *Nation*, April 18, 1942, pp. 454–456.

White, William L. "Report on the Russians." *Reader's Digest* 45 (December 1944): 115–122.

Willen, Paul. "Who 'Collaborated' with Russia?" *Antioch Review* 14 (September 1954): 259–283.

Williams, Maynard Owen. "Mother Volga Defends Her Own." *National Geographic Magazine* 82 (December 1942): 793–811.

Wood, John Perry. "Mr. Truman 'Not Alarmed.'" *Los Angeles Times*, March 17, 1946, p. 4.

Japan: Unanswered Challenge, 1931–1941

NORMAN A. GRAEBNER

JAPAN'S CHALLENGE to U.S. foreign policy during the decade before Pearl Harbor was unique only in matters of time and place. In nature and quality, that challenge, no less than the response it produced in Washington, created tensions not unlike those that non–status-quo powers traditionally exert on the international order, and especially on that country which regards itself as the special guarantor of that order. What rendered the Japanese assault on established international relationships embarrassingly troublesome for the United States, however, was the total lack of symmetry between Japanese and American interests in the Far East. For the United States, the status of that region was of marginal concern; for Japan, it raised questions not only of national self-esteem but also of national survival. Thus, to Japan, the pursuit of a new order in East Asia never excluded the use of force; to the United States, the maintenance of the old order was scarcely worth the price of war. Still Washington officials, for reasons of their own, refused to the end to compromise the old order in the interest of peace. It was not strange, therefore, that war came to the United States in December 1941 by inadvertence. Because of the absence of any clear American interest in China worth defending, it could hardly have been otherwise.

Tokyo's rejection of the post-Versailles order in the Far East was profound. Japanese expansionism was bound up in Japan's history, its geographical position, its population problems in relation to its land areas, its food supply, and the availability of raw materials for industrial expansion. Japan's scarcely concealed ambitions toward China reflected both insecurity and economic necessity. What disturbed Tokyo especially was the perennial danger that the Western powers would enlarge their presence in China at the expense of Chinese integrity and Japanese security. "Japan is an island nation," admitted Viscount Ishii Kikujiro, Japan's noted statesman. "But her distance from the continent of Asia is so small that she cannot be indifferent to what happens in Korea, Manchuria and Siberia."[1]

Japan's direct designs for China reflected fundamentally the needs of the Japanese population. American writer Arthur Bullard described the essence of Japanese expansionism toward the mainland when he wrote in *Harper's Monthly Magazine*: "However threatening Japanese ambitions may be to us, they have to face a worse menace at home. They have a baby-peril, more dangerous than Oriental immigration ever was to us. Each new child born to them means the desperate pressure of over-population."[2] Japan faced three choices: famine, emigration, or industrial expansion. There were no others. It was certain that the Japanese government would never accept the first alternative and that no

[1] Viscount Ishii Kikujiro, "The Permanent Bases of Japanese Foreign Policy," *Foreign Affairs* 11 (January 1933): 224.
[2] Arthur Bullard, "Expanding Japan," *Harper's Monthly Magazine* 139 (November 1919): 857–858.

Western country would willingly eliminate its policies of exclusion aimed at the Asian peoples. Japan, therefore, could sustain its growing population only with expanding industry and commerce.

Japanese industrialization raised the fundamental question of the distribution of the world's land and natural resources, for Japan lacked the three essentials of oil, iron, and coal. Ultimately, Asian stability would require a more equitable distribution of territory and resources throughout the Far East. But to satisfy its immediate industrial needs, Japan demanded the opportunity to share in the development of China's natural resources, especially those in Manchuria, whether China consented or not. General Sadao Araki, Japanese minister of war in the early thirties, declared that, since mankind had "the right to live upon the earth," no country with abundant resources had the right to deny them to another country insufficiently endowed by nature.[3] Japan's special economic ambitions in China carried with them the self-assigned responsibility for leading China into a new age of economic efficiency and political stability.[4]

In large measure the concept of a "Japanese Monroe Doctrine" embodied Tokyo's claims to special or paramount interests in the Far East. It explained both Japan's objectives in China and its attitudes toward the Western powers in the Far East. Japan's Monroe Doctrine, like that of the United States, asserted Tokyo's special claims to regional leadership. "From our point of view," observed Ishii, "Japan possesses interests superior to other Powers in China as a whole, especially in the contiguous regions, much as the position of [the United States] in the Western Hemisphere."[5] Japan demanded recognition of

[3] Quoted in George H. Blakeslee, "The Japanese Monroe Doctrine," *Foreign Affairs* 11 (July 1933): 676.

[4] Ibid., p. 673.

[5] Ibid., p. 671.

its superior rights and its dominant power in the western Pacific as well as the international courtesy and the advantages that accrued generally to the world's modern, progressive, and efficient countries. Japan viewed itself, moreover, as the one country that, by reducing Western influence in East Asia, could establish the principle of "Asia for the Asiatics."

But nowhere could Japan alter the status quo in East and Southeast Asia without challenging a wide spectrum of Western possessions and treaty rights, which the non-Asian powers would never willingly surrender. The Great War had eliminated Russia and Germany from the main currents of Asian affairs; it had weakened Britain and France beyond recall. Thus, after Versailles, the United States alone possessed sufficient power in the Pacific to curtail Japanese expansion. Japan confronted the United States with two inescapable alternatives in the Far East: either this country would accept a dominant economic and political role for Japan in East Asia or it would fight to prevent it. Bullard defined the American choice in such terms as early as 1919. "Unless we want to 'smash' Japan," he warned, "we must facilitate her commercial access to China."[6] Either response to Japanese expansion—and there was really no third—exceeded the military and political limits of an acceptable American policy. Still, as early as the Manchurian crisis of 1931, Washington officials searched for the means of escape from the cruel dilemmas posed by Japanese behavior.

Manchuria emerged as the key to Japanese industrial expansion. Under Japanese control, that region served as a minimal barrier to Russian encroachment along the Asian littoral. Beyond that, Manchuria possessed the natural riches that Formosa and Korea had failed to supply. With time, it promised to

---

[6] Bullard, "Expanding Japan," pp. 865–866.

furnish much of the food and raw materials necessary for Japan's economic existence. So successful had been Japanese investments and industrial leadership in developing the Manchurian economy that by 1931 almost thirty million people, overwhelmingly Chinese, lived in the three Japanese-controlled provinces. But it was becoming increasingly clear that the Chinese migration was evolving into a massive effort to drive the Japanese out of the region. Convinced that Chinese nationalism and antiforeignism endangered Japan's privileged position in Manchuria, Japanese officials in the province determined to exploit the Mukden incident of September 1931 occasioned by the alleged destruction of track along the Japanese-controlled South Manchurian Railway to convert Manchuria into a Japanese dependency.

When news of the Mukden clash reached Washington, President Herbert Hoover and his advisers revealed no inclination to escape responsibility for what occurred. Their response to Manchuria established the post-Versailles pattern of American behavior toward unwanted changes in international life. What disturbed Washington in the Japanese assault on Manchuria was not the violation of this nation's vital interests. No major U.S. official, either in Washington or in the Far East, ever defined any American interest in Asia sufficiently important to justify war. What the Japanese assault endangered was the credibility of the entire post-Versailles international treaty structure that supposedly had eliminated the employment of force in relations among states. The United States had not entered the League of Nations, but it had assumed the lead in negotiating both the Nine Power Pact of 1922 and the Kellogg-Briand Peace Pact of 1928. For Washington, these two treaties safeguarded the world's peace, not by the exercise of power, but by the promise of each signatory to refrain from activities that would infringe on the rights of other countries. Japan, in signing them, had agreed to share the responsibility for maintaining the peace of Asia. At stake in Manchuria, therefore, was the stability of the post-Versailles international order. Clearly, the United States, as the most powerful country with interests in China, would not ignore the events in Manchuria.

This American devotion to the treaty system reduced U.S. purpose in the Manchurian crisis to the simplistic quest of obtaining Japan's compliance with its international obligations. Such an approach, if successful, would enable Washington to bridge the gap between its determination to uphold the status quo in the Far East and its determination to avoid a war over the future of China. Stanley K. Hornbeck, chief of the Division of Far Eastern Affairs, advised the Hoover administration to base any protests to Tokyo, not on the principle of the Open Door and U.S. interests in China, but on the question of international peace. U.S. Minister to China Nelson T. Johnson admitted his indifference to Manchuria's future but not to the future of world peace, which, he wrote, demanded that all nations accept their commitments under the Kellogg Pact and the League of Nations. "The fate of Manchuria," he warned the State Department in November 1931, "is of secondary importance compared to the fate of the League."[7] League proponents found immense satisfaction in Hoover's initial decision of October to cooperate with the League.

Secretary of State Henry L. Stimson readily agreed with Hornbeck and Johnson that U.S. interests in China were insignificant when contrasted to the American stake in the world's peace structure. On October 9, Stimson warned President Hoover at a cabinet meeting against placing the United States in

[7] Johnson to Peck, November 3, 1931, in Roland N. Stromberg, *Collective Security and American Foreign Policy*, p. 68.

a humiliating position should Japan refuse to honor its signatures on the Nine Power and Kellogg treaties. Then in his diary he recorded the essential role of the peace treaties in the assumptions and purposes of U.S. foreign policy:

The question of the "scraps of paper" is a pretty crucial one. We have nothing but "scraps of paper." This fight has come on in the worst part of the world for peace treaties. The peace treaties of modern Europe made out by the Western nations of the world do no more fit the three great races of Russia, Japan, and China, who are meeting in Manchuria, than, as I put it to the Cabinet, a stovepipe hat would fit an African savage. Nevertheless they are parties to these treaties and the whole world looks on to see whether the treaties are good for anything or not, and if we lie down and treat them like scraps of paper nothing will happen, and in the future the peace movement will receive a blow that it will not recover from for a long time.[8]

For Stimson, peace had become indivisible. Japanese aggression, if unchallenged, would destroy the credibility of the entire system of collective security built essentially on the single force of world opinion. Stimson would, therefore, demand that Japan, as a signatory of the Nine Power and Kellogg pacts, sacrifice its interests and ambitions to the higher good of world peace, which underlay the interests of the United States. Hoover confirmed this American response to the Manchurian crisis in a memorandum presented to his cabinet in mid-October. Japanese behavior, he said, was outrageous—a moral affront to the United States. But he reminded the cabinet that this nation carried no obligation to maintain peace among other states by force. Both the Nine Power and Kellogg pacts, he said, were "solely moral instruments based upon the hope that peace in the world can be held by the rectitude of nations and enforced

[8] Henry L. Stimson and McGeorge Bundy, *On Active Service in Peace and War*, p. 233.

solely by the moral reprobation of the world."[9] If Japan imperiled no fundamental American interests, the United States still had the "moral obligation to use every influence short of war to have the treaties upheld or limited by mutual agreement." Again, in his December 1931 message to Congress, the president acknowledged U.S. responsibility for the integrity of China under the Nine Power and Kellogg treaties.[10] For Hoover and Stimson, it appeared essential that the United States make its will effective in Japanese-Chinese relations without resorting to either economic or military sanctions.

But how could they achieve their purpose? Japan, it was clear, was preparing to establish permanent control over Manchuria. As early as November, Stimson contemplated a resort to moral sanctions. He concluded that month that it might be wise "to outlaw Japan and let her sizzle [under a Chinese boycott] and all the moral pressure of the world."[11] Early in December, Hoover suggested to the cabinet that the United States propose to the League that its members refuse to recognize any changes in Manchuria that resulted from violations of the Kellogg Pact. Stimson himself resurrected the Wilsonian doctrine of non-recognition when he wrote to Charles G. Dawes, the U.S. observer at the League, "We do not see how we can do anything more ourselves . . . than to announce our disapproval and to announce that we will not recognize any treaties which may be forced by Japan under the pressure of military occupation."[12] Stimson recognized both the need and the limitations of non-recognition as the means for reinforcing the treaty system. "If the fruits of aggression should be recognized," he admitted,

[9] For the text of Hoover's cabinet memorandum see William Starr Myers, *The Foreign Policies of Herbert Hoover, 1929–1933*, pp. 156–159.

[10] Ray Lyman Wilbur and Arthur Mastick Hyde (eds.), *The Hoover Policies*, pp. 601–602.

[11] Quoted in Stromberg, *Collective Security*, p. 77.

[12] Ibid.

"the whole theory of the Kellogg Pact would be repudiated, and the world would be at once returned to the point of recognizing war as a legitimate instrument of national policy. Nonrecognition might not prevent aggression, but recognition would give it outright approval."[13]

On January 7, 1932, Stimson, in his first effort to terminate Japanese expansion through moral sanctions, sent identical notes to Japan and China declaring that this nation could not "admit the legality of any situation *de facto* nor does it intend to recognize any treaty or agreement entered into between those Governments" that might impair either the treaty rights of the United States or the territorial and administrative integrity of the Republic of China.[14] Both Hoover and Stimson believed that the note would be effective. Hoover declared in January that it had mobilized world opinion against Japan and would stand as one of the country's great state papers. Much of the American press agreed. The *Providence Journal* lauded the note as one of "clear and far-reaching importance in the history of twentieth-century diplomacy."[15] Only a minority warned that the note would not serve the cause of peace at all. The *Chicago Daily News* admitted that the reassertion of American principles might appear harmless enough. "But pin-prick notes," ran its conclusion, "irritate the sensitive and proud Japanese, and stiffen the attitude of the dominant military clique. China's ultimate interests may be served better by a policy of patience and discretion, by overlooking Japan's inconsistencies, and letting it restore order and security throughout Manchuria."[16] Even the U.S. ambassador to Tokyo, W. Cameron Forbes, found little in Stimson's verbal toughness that would stop Japan or serve the interests of the

---

[13] Stimson and Bundy, *On Active Service*, p. 235.
[14] Ibid., pp. 235–236.
[15] Quoted in *Literary Digest*, January 23, 1932, p. 5.
[16] Ibid., p. 6.

United States. To Forbes, the paper treaties of the twenties had lost their relevance; rhetorical recriminations based on such documents would only aggravate tensions in the Pacific.

Japan, undaunted by Stimson's moral strictures, continued to exert pressure on China. Finally, on January 28, 1932, the Japanese invaded Shanghai. Again Stimson was outraged. He hoped, he confided to his diary, that the Japanese would not withdraw until the United States could pass firm judgment against the new aggression.[17] "As I reflected upon it," he recalled later, "it seemed to me that in future years I should not like to face a verdict of history to the effect that a government to which I belonged had failed to express itself adequately upon such a situation."[18] On February 16 the League Council supported the nonrecognition doctrine and called upon Japan to fulfill its obligations under the Nine Power Treaty. Thereupon Stimson leveled his second moral blast at Japan in the form of an open letter to Senator William E. Borah, dated February 23, 1932. Nothing, declared Stimson, had occurred to challenge the validity of either the Nine Power or the Kellogg pact. These two documents, he reminded Japan, "represent independent but harmonious steps taken for the purpose of aligning the conscience and public opinion of the world in favor of a system of orderly development by the law of nations, including a settlement of all controversies by methods of justice and peace instead of by arbitrary force." Stimson warned Tokyo that nonrecognition, if adopted by the other powers, "will eventually lead to the restoration to China of rights and titles of which she may have been deprived."[19] Never before had Stimson made such extrav-

[17] See Richard N. Current, "The Stimson Doctrine and the Hoover Doctrine," *American Historical Review* 59 (April 1954): 529.

[18] Henry L. Stimson, *The Far Eastern Crisis: Recollections and Observations*, p. 157.

[19] *Papers Relating to the Foreign Relations of the United States. Japan, 1931–1941*, I, 87.

agant claims for the coercive power of nonrecognition. Still Japan continued to move. During March the Japanese smuggled Henry Pu Yi, the former emperor of China, into Manchuria and installed him as head of the new Japanese-controlled puppet state of Manchukuo.

Nonrecognition, as an ineffective sanction, gave the administration the remaining choice of resorting to arms or acknowledging the failure of its moral rhetoric. Stimson again escaped the first alternative with a further attempt at moral pressure. Addressing the New York Council on Foreign Relations in August, he implored the nations to join the United States in strengthening the Kellogg-Briand Pact by adding their voices of condemnation to that expressed by this country in January. "Moral disapproval," he said, "when it becomes the disapproval of the whole world, takes on a significance hitherto unknown in international law. For never before has international opinion been so organized and mobilized."[20] Stimson received the customary adulation for his peaceful disposition of the Japanese problem. The *New York World Telegram* praised the Hoover-Stimson doctrine of nonrecognition as "the most important international step taken by the United States since the World War."[21] Writing in the April 1933 issue of *Foreign Affairs*, Stimson asserted that the Hoover administration, in supporting the Kellogg Pact, had made it "a living force of law in the world."[22]

Thus Washington managed in 1932 both to avoid war in the Pacific and to escape any admission of failure in the Manchurian crisis. For that reason, the Hoover-Stimson doctrine emerged as

[20] Stimson and Bundy, *On Active Service*, p. 259; *Literary Digest*, August 20, 1932, p. 6.

[21] *Literary Digest*, August 20, 1932, p. 6.

[22] Henry L. Stimson, "Bases of American Foreign Policy during the Past Four Years," *Foreign Affairs* 11 (April 1933): 394, 396.

an astonishingly attractive formula domestically. But the doctrine was scarcely promising abroad. It had not stopped Japan. And it had nailed the American preference for the status quo in the Far East, not to American power, but to the sanctity of an outmoded treaty structure. Washington's military abstention from the Manchurian affair illustrated clearly that Japan had not challenged any immediate U.S. interest. But the Hoover administration, by defining Japanese aggression as a threat to world peace, permitted the United States only a temporary escape from the continuing Far Eastern crisis. By preventing Japan from solidifying its gains through universally recognized agreements, the United States would one day emerge as Japan's enemy and the major source of its ultimate frustration. The Hoover-Stimson doctrine, designed to avoid a Japanese-American confrontation in Asia, rendered war inevitable.

Still the Hoover-Stimson doctrine appeared so laudable in precept, so promising in action, that Franklin D. Roosevelt accepted it without modification as the essence of his Far Eastern policy. Following a long conversation with Stimson at Hyde Park, Roosevelt agreed on January 17, 1933, that "American foreign policy must *uphold* the *sanctity* of international treaties. This is the cornerstone on which all relations between nations must rest."[23] Throughout Roosevelt's first term, the Japanese

---

[23] Edgar B. Nixon (ed.), *Franklin D. Roosevelt and Foreign Affairs*, I, 4. Roosevelt's advisers, Raymond Moley and Rexford G. Tugwell, warned Roosevelt that his January 17, 1933, statement ran the risk of placing the United States in an impossible position in the Far East. The president answered that he sympathized with the Chinese people and therefore had no choice but to go along with Stimson on the Japanese question. Moley observed: "That was all. It was so simple, so incredible, there could be no answer." See Raymond Moley, *After Seven Years*, pp. 94–95; Bernard Sternsher, "The Stimson Doctrine: F.D.R. *versus* Moley and Tugwell," *Pacific Historical Review* 31 (August 1962): 281–289.

continued to make clear their rejection of the Far Eastern treaty structure. Tokyo officials warned repeatedly that Japan alone carried the responsibility for peace and order in East Asia. No country, declared Amau Eiji, a Japanese Foreign Ministry spokesman, in April 1934, could share that responsibility but China. "We oppose, therefore," he warned, "any attempt on the part of China to avail herself of the influence of any other country to resist Japan."[24] Whatever the level of their conflicting interests in the Orient, the United States and Japan were clearly on a collision course.

Roosevelt and Secretary of State Cordell Hull adopted the Republican formula of nonrecognition with little regard for its consequences. Their automatic rejection of Japanese gains eliminated the need for either an understanding of Japanese expansionism or an accurate measurement of U.S. interests in the Far East. In practice, Hull would avoid direct military involvement in the Pacific even while he sought, through the constant reiteration of American principles of peaceful change, the total capitulation of Japan to Chinese will. To close the gap between these two fundamentally incongruous objectives, he would exhort Japan to live peacefully by limiting its demands to what all parties in China would accept through negotiation alone.

Meanwhile, China carried the burden of protecting what remained of the Open Door. It was better that China suffer, observed Hornbeck in February 1934, for any settlement would compel China to recognize Japanese-imposed change in direct defiance of the Nine Power Pact.[25] Scrapping the Open Door in China, moreover, would compel the United States to give up its treaty rights. "If we did this without making an announcement,"

[24] *New York Times*, April 21, 1934.

[25] Hornbeck Memorandum, May 9, 1933, President's Secretary's File (hereafter cited as PSF): China, 1933–1936, Box 3, Franklin D. Roosevelt Library, Hyde Park, New York, hereafter cited as FDRL.

ran a State Department memorandum of January 1935, "we would produce all sorts of misunderstanding and confusion. If we did it with an announcement, such announcement would be tantamount to a declaration that, so far as we are concerned, Japan may do as she pleases in and with regard to China."[26] Compromise would demonstrate a lack of moral firmness and thus become an invitation to disaster. Even while the Roosevelt administration revealed no intention of fighting Japan, it viewed the United States as the special guarantor of the status quo in the Far East.

War returned to the Orient on July 7, 1937, when a regiment of Japanese troops on maneuvers near the Marco Polo Bridge outside Peking exchanged shots with local Chinese soldiers. Tokyo seized this armed clash, much as it had the Mukden incident five years earlier, to wrest another body of special concessions from the Chinese government. Hull's response to this crisis was almost identical to that of Stimson. On July 16 he released a statement to the press that reaffirmed this country's devotion to the treaty structure. "We advocate," wrote Hull, "adjustment of problems in international relations by processes of peaceful negotiation and agreement. We advocate faithful observance of international agreements. Upholding the principle of the sanctity of treaties, we believe in modification of provisions of treaties . . . by orderly processes carried out in a spirit of mutual helpfulness and accommodation."[27] These principles again eliminated every possibility that Washington might come to terms with Japan over the future of China.

Roosevelt's famed Quarantine Speech in Chicago on October 5, 1937, bespoke a stronger response to Japanese aggression,

[26] Memorandum of January 3, 1935, PSF: Diplomatic Correspondence, Japan, Box 13, FDRL.

[27] *Papers Relating to the Foreign Relations of the United States, 1937*, I, 699–700.

including a suggestion of collective security. Still that speech scarcely altered the quality of American policy in the Far East. "It seems to be unfortunately true," Roosevelt warned, "that the epidemic of world lawlessness is spreading. . . . When an epidemic of physical disease starts to spread, the community approves and joins in a quarantine of the patients in order to protect the health of the community against the spread of the disease."[28] Roosevelt's open partisanship aroused the nation's isolationists; never again would they trust him. But his speech failed to create the foundation for a national policy. It did not define U.S. interests anywhere except in terms of the status quo. Peace-loving nations, he said, "must work together for the triumph of law and moral principles in order that peace, justice, and confidence may prevail in the world." Nor did the president suggest any body of means that might be effective. He favored, he told newsmen, a program that might create a stronger neutrality. Two weeks after the speech, he handed adviser Norman Davis a statement that suggested "the possibility of a constructive program in which a group of neutrals, acting together, but without threat of force, might make their influence felt."[29]

On October 6 the League of Nations invited its members who were also signatories of the Nine Power Pact to call an international conference to settle the Sino-Japanese dispute. Roosevelt suggested Brussels, but refused to permit the Belgian government to send out invitations in his name. The president selected Norman Davis to head the American delegation. Brussels confronted Washington with another policy crisis. Roosevelt's goal of halting Japan had no relationship to the means

[28] *Peace and War: United States Foreign Policy, 1931–1941*, pp. 383–387.

[29] Dorothy Borg, *The United States and the Far Eastern Crisis of 1933–1938*, pp. 381–386. This is a superb account of Roosevelt and the Quarantine Speech.

available to him. Unable to act, yet required to do so, Roosevelt retreated to the Hoover-Stimson formula of resorting to moral sanctions that had permitted Washington to escape a similar dilemma in 1932. The president instructed Davis to reject either joint action with the League or a British-led quest for collective security. Instead, said Roosevelt, the delegates should pose questions to Japan "which would become increasingly embarrassing and which would continue to mobilize public opinion and moral force."[30] For Hull, the conference would become the agency "for educating public opinion and bringing to bear upon Japan all possible moral pressure."[31]

Even before the Brussels Conference opened on November 3, the delegates were seeking an excuse to terminate the discussions. Davis stood alone. The smaller European powers with interests in the Far East were too powerless to take any stand against Japan. Britain, France, Russia, and China had no interest in condemnatory resolutions that they knew would be ineffective. The Japanese made it clear that they would not attend the conference at all. Following the opening statements at Brussels, Western leaders generally, as well as much of the press, found the American program of stopping Japan with an aroused world opinion untenable. Davis's reports dwelt on the almost universal rejection of U.S. policy. Still Washington would not be dissuaded. Undersecretary Sumner Welles reminded Davis of American objectives. "Every effort," he instructed Davis, "is to be made to rally moral opinion in every other country of the world in favor of the principles embodied in the Nine Power Treaty. . . . The whole premise of the government in going to the Brussels Conference was the keeping alive . . . of international law and morality."[32]

---

[30] Memorandum in PSF: State Department, 1937, Box 32, FDRL.
[31] Cordell Hull, *Memoirs*, I, 552.
[32] *Foreign Relations, 1937*, IV, 154–155.

Despite his efforts to impose the U.S. formula on the conference, Davis could stem neither the cynicism of the press nor the resentment of the other delegations. The British, he informed Hull, demanded strong action or the immediate termination of the conference. For the London delegation, there was no merit or dignity in a mere statement of principles. Hull countered by informing Davis that he could best relieve the criticism of American leadership with "a strong reaffirmation of the principles which should underlie international relationships."[33] But time had run out; Hull agreed to an adjournment. On November 24, three weeks after it opened, the Brussels Conference adopted its resolutions and disbanded. Davis reminded the disillusioned Chinese that the powers "had rendered a real service to China, particularly in reaffirming their adherence to the principles of the Nine Power Treaty."[34] For Stimson, the Brussels Conference comprised a grave and inescapable challenge to American leadership. It was essential, he reminded Roosevelt, that the United States both uphold its principles at Brussels and find a genuine solution to the Far Eastern problem. Nothing less than universal peace and freedom was at stake in China. Roosevelt and Hull admitted the gravity of the crisis as well as their inability to offer a solution. "As for the answer," wrote Roosevelt, "frankly, we have not found it."[35]

Following the failure at Brussels, Japan continued to confront Washington with only two realistic alternatives: to accept a larger role for Japan in the affairs of the Orient or to terminate Japan's expanding war in China with force. For Roosevelt, neither alternative was acceptable. To stop Japan would require

[33] Ibid., pp. 184–185, 194–196, 225–226.
[34] Ibid., pp. 231–233.
[35] Stimson to Roosevelt, November 15, 1937, Roosevelt to Hull, November 22, 1937, Roosevelt to Stimson, November 24, 1937, President's Personal File 20 (hereafter cited as PPF), FDRL.

a military price far out of proportion to American interests in China. To abjure the traditional guardianship of the Open Door and the treaty system in China would demand a political price equally unacceptable. Hull explained simply in January 1938 that "the Government of the United States . . . has asked and is asking that the rights of the United States . . . be respected, and at the same time it has sought and is seeking to avoid involvement of this country in the disputes of other countries."[36] Even while the administration attempted to escape any military involvement in the Far East, it remained, by choice, the final arbiter in Chinese affairs. As long as Roosevelt could tolerate the Japanese assault on American citizens and property in China, he could extend his formula of moral involvement without military commitment into an indefinite future.

On November 3, 1938, the Japanese government promulgated its ultimate design for a "New Order in East Asia." That day, Premier Konoe Fumimaro explained in a radio broadcast: "Japan desires to build up a stabilized Far East by cooperating with the Chinese people who have awakened to the needs of self-determination as an Oriental race. . . . History shows that Japan, Manchukuo and China are so related to each other that they must bind themselves closely together in a common mission for the establishment of peace and order in the Far East."[37] For the United States, the choices in the Far East were narrowing perceptibly. Still Roosevelt refused to confront the Japanese with either threatened sanctions or a willingness to acknowledge Japan's economic and psychological dilemmas, which drove that country along its expansionist course. Instead, U.S. Ambassador

[36] Hull's statement of January 15, 1938, quoted in William Crane Johnstone, *The United States and Japan's New Order*, p. 254.

[37] Quoted in Chihiro Hosoya, "Miscalculations in Deterrent Policy: Japanese-U.S. Relations, 1938–1941," *Journal of Peace Research* (Oslo), no. 2 (1968), p. 113.

to Tokyo Joseph C. Grew complained to the Japanese Foreign Office that Japan attempted to create its new order, not in accordance with its treaty obligations, but "by methods of its own selection, regardless of treaty pledges and the established rights of other powers concerned." Changing conditions in the Orient demanded new agreements, Grew admitted, but these required "orderly processes of negotiation and agreement among the parties thereto."[38] Opposed by a treaty structure changeable only by general agreement, Japan faced the simple choice of limiting its status in China to its treaty rights or extending its war across China into an unknown future.

To stop the drift in U.S. policy, which refused either to undo or to accept Japan's struggle for a new order in East Asia, Roosevelt's friends and advisers urged him to consider some form of coercion against Japan. This group agreed overwhelmingly that economic sanctions would be the surest and safest means of forcing Japan to capitulate. In November 1938, Admiral William D. Leahy reminded Roosevelt that Japan depended on open sea lanes for its vital commerce. "Any threat against these lines of communication," Leahy predicted, "will have a profound effect on her attitude of mind regarding the settlement of the present controversy."[39] That month, a Roosevelt correspondent, Marine Captain Evans F. Carlson, wrote from China, "If the flow of oil and munitions to Japan was stopped she could not continue this conflict for another six months."[40] Hornbeck urged the administration to exert economic pressure on Tokyo by terminating the U.S.-Japanese commercial treaty of 1911, thereby placing U.S. trade with Japan on a day-to-day

[38] Grew to Arita, December 30, 1938, *Peace and War*, pp. 441–447.
[39] For a similar view see Irving Fisher to Roosevelt, August 20, 1937, PPF 431, FDRL.
[40] Carlson to Miss LeHand, November 15, 1938, PPF 4951, FDRL.

basis. In December 1938, Hornbeck insisted that U.S. economic retaliation against Japan would produce rapid and significant revisions in Japan's new order.[41]

Still convinced that no American interest in China was worth a war in the Pacific, Roosevelt hesitated to antagonize Tokyo with either financial aid to China or commercial restrictions against Japan. Finally, in December 1938, he responded to Secretary of the Treasury Henry Morgenthau's arguments favoring financial aid to China with a $25 million loan. Then during January 1939, he initiated a "moral embargo" on airplanes and parts to Japan. In February he ordered a cessation of credits. Responding to the mounting domestic pressure, now centering in the Congress, the State Department, on July 26, 1939, formally notified Tokyo of the abrogation of the 1911 treaty. Six months later—on January 26, 1940—the treaty would cease to be effective. Friends of the administration were delighted. "Warm congratulations on your notice," William G. McAdoo wired the president on July 27. "This ought to have a great and beneficial effect."[42] Admiral Richard E. Byrd commended the president: "History will, without a doubt, show the great effectiveness of the very firm stand you have taken in the direction of international law and order."[43] Even the threat of economic sanctions, prophesied Evans Carlson, would halt Japan without war.

Roosevelt's preparations for economic sanctions began to separate those advisers who believed that such sanctions would terminate Japanese aggression from those who warned that such policies would drive Japan into new forms of expansion and

[41] *Foreign Relations, 1938*, III, 425–427.

[42] McAdoo to Roosevelt, July 27, 1939, Roosevelt to McAdoo, August 3, 1939, PPF 308, FDRL.

[43] Byrd to Roosevelt, July 31, 1939, Roosevelt to Byrd, August 2, 1939, PPF 201, FDRL.

probably into war with the United States. In January 1940, Stimson urged an embargo on war materials against Japan. This, he said, would entail no risk inasmuch as Japan would avoid war with the United States. Frank Knox, publisher of the *Chicago Daily News*, assured the president that Japan's position was weakening. "The tendency," he wrote, "is a healthy one which will continue if Uncle Sam stays tough and the Chinese remain uncooperative. The only hope for a return to peace and sanity in the Far East is the continuance of this trend."[44] Within the administration, those who most notably favored the hard line were Morgenthau, Secretary of the Interior Harold L. Ickes, and Hornbeck. The president strengthened this group when, in 1940, he appointed Stimson and Knox to the cabinet as the new secretaries of war and the navy. Stimson wrote shortly after assuming his new office, "The only way to treat Japan is not to give her anything."[45]

Others were not convinced. Grew warned Roosevelt in November 1939 that an embargo against Japan would produce a total disintegration in U.S.-Japanese relations. From Tokyo, Assistant Secretary of State Francis Sayre warned Washington that an embargo would inflame Japanese opinion and render a Far Eastern settlement almost impossible. Rather it would compel Tokyo to pursue its new order with greater determination.[46] Those in the State Department who shared the conviction that economic pressure on Japan would produce war rather than capitulation were Hull, Welles, and Maxwell Hamilton of the Far East Division. If these men did not favor extensive concessions to Japan, they agreed generally that U.S. interests in the

[44] Knox to Roosevelt, January 23, 1940, PSF: Frank Knox, Box 28, FDRL.

[45] Quoted in Hosoya, "Miscalculations in Deterrent Policy," p. 106.

[46] Grew to Roosevelt, November 6, 1939, PSF: Diplomatic Correspondence, Japan, Box 13, FDRL; Sayre Memorandum, May 1, 1940, ibid.

Far East were too negligible to necessitate a drastic response to Japan's encroachments on the mainland.

As late as 1940, the United States had offered little tangible aid to China. The American conception of national interest had been bound less to Chinese integrity than to the integrity of the treaty system—a broader but more abstract concern that had demanded no real response to Japanese aggression. Until mid-1940, U.S. officials assumed that Chinese resistance, added to the threat of economic sanctions, would ultimately place limits on Japanese ambitions. Suddenly, Washington discovered too late that Japanese expansion had entered a new, more threatening phase. The German offensive in Europe during May and June 1940 rendered the Dutch, French, and British empires in Southeast Asia vulnerable to Japanese encroachments. Unable to negotiate a settlement with China, the Japanese moved to consolidate their position by controlling the southern approaches to that country. The threatened embargo on oil, moreover, focused Japanese attention on the oil resources of the Dutch East Indies. With France's defeat, Tokyo demanded that Britain stop all shipments to China. At the same time, Tokyo extracted the promise of a million tons of oil from the Dutch and pressed France for the right to occupy northern Indochina.

Japan's burgeoning assault on the European empires in Southeast Asia broadened the American interest from concern for the treaty system in China to the defense of the East Asian balance of power. Congress responded in July with the National Defense Act, which gave the president the authority to place under license arms, munitions, critical and strategic raw materials, airplane parts, optical instruments, and metal-working machinery. To moderate the impact of such restrictions on Japan the president omitted oil and scrap iron from his order. But later, in July, under pressure from Stimson, Knox, Morgenthau, and Hornbeck, the president added oil and scrap iron to the export license system. State Department officers, led by Hamilton, gained a compromise that limited restrictions to aviation fuel, lubricants, and heavy melting iron and steel scrap. Finally, as Japan continued its thrusts into Southeast Asia, the president, in September, terminated the sale of scrap iron and steel to Japan. But clearly such pressures only accelerated the Japanese drive into Southeast Asia. Then on September 27, 1940, Japan signed the Tripartite Pact with Germany and Italy.

Until that moment, Washington had never regarded China as an ally. United States officials had scarcely treated Chinese resistance as an element in this country's security. But Japan's new identification with the Axis powers in Europe—a genuine diplomatic blunder—transformed Japan into a potential enemy and China into another ally fighting the totalitarian powers. Japanese action, at least to American interventionists, brought the Pacific war into the Atlantic. Clark Eichelberger, director of the Committee to Defend America, observed in October, "Britain and China in the Pacific, with Britain in the Atlantic, now constitute our first lines of defense."[47] Grew argued against this tendency to attribute like motives and characteristics to the Japanese and German governments. For him it was essential that Washington distinguish between its immediate and long-term goals in the Far East.[48] To avoid war in the Pacific and to counter Japan's advance into Southeast Asia, the United States, he believed, could well continue to tolerate the Japanese occupation of China.

Unconcerned with such distinctions, Roosevelt cautiously es-

[47] Warren I. Cohen, "From Contempt to Containment: Cycles in American Attitudes toward China," in *Twentieth-Century American Foreign Policy*, ed. John Braeman, Robert H. Bremner, and David Brody, p. 553.

[48] Grew's dispatch of September 12, 1940, in Joseph C. Grew, *Turbulent Era: A Diplomatic Record of Forty Years, 1904–1945*, ed. Walter Johnson, II, 1224–1229.

calated the U.S. involvement in the Pacific. On November 30 he
placed another $100 million at Chiang Kai-shek's disposal. Aid
to China now replaced the former trade with Japan. In December, Roosevelt dispatched ships and planes to the Philippines
under the principle, as Hull explained it, "of letting [the Japa-
nese] guess as to when and in what set of circumstances we
would fight."[49] As late as January 1941, the president had established no goals in the Far East that reflected the nation's
minimal interests, its lack of military preparations, and its determination to avoid war. Still, the United States would no
longer accept China's sorrows passively. China's status as an ally,
moreover, would reinforce Washington's determination to encourage no Far Eastern settlement at China's expense.

Admiral Nomura Kichisaburo, who arrived in Washington as
Japanese ambassador in February 1941, had no chance against
Washington's perennial determination to place its hopes for
peace in the Far East on the altar of diplomatic inflexibility.
Hull reminded Nomura what the United States expected of
Japan on April 16, when he presented to the Japanese ambassador his four principles, which became the final stand of the U.S.
government: "(1) respect for the territorial integrity and the
sovereignty of each and all nations; (2) support of the principle
of non-interference in the internal affairs of other countries;
(3) support of the principle of equality, including equality of
commercial opportunity; (4) non-disturbance of the *status quo*
in the Pacific except as the *status quo* may be altered by peaceful
means."[50] For Hull, the American conditions for peace in the
Pacific seemed reasonable enough; for the Japanese government,
as its response of May 12 made clear, they demanded little less
than a Japanese capitulation. Tokyo requested above all that the

49 Hull, *Memoirs*, I, 915.
50 Memorandum of conversations between Hull and Nomura, April
16, 1941, PSF: Diplomatic Correspondence, Japan, Box 13, FDRL.

United States cooperate in establishing peace in China by requesting Chiang to negotiate under the threat of the discontinuance of all American aid should he refuse. But Japan asked also the right to negotiate on the basis of its power and efficiency as well as the resumption of normal trade relations with the United States.[51] Hull rejected the Japanese formula because it in no measure guaranteed a peace based on his four principles. Japan would have peace on Chinese terms or not at all.

Japan responded with the determination to establish its Greater East Asian Co-Prosperity Sphere and occupy southern Indochina, whatever the obstacles involved. Roosevelt countered with a promise that if Japan would refrain from advancing into Indochina he would seek a multinational declaration establishing Indochina's neutralization.[52] When he received no response, the president, on July 26, issued an executive order freezing Japanese assets in the United States and thereby effectively terminated all U.S. commercial and financial relations with Japan. This move, at last, stopped the export of oil to Japan. Much of Washington and the press, thoroughly attuned by mid-1941 to the notion that the inflexible rejection of all Japanese gains was the surest guarantee of peace, lauded the president's decision. Assured that Japan would not fight, Roosevelt failed to attach any objectives, achievable through diplomacy, to his embargo. Thus U.S. economic sanctions, effective beyond anticipation, would force Japan, with only a year's supply of oil on hand, into a quick capitulation or an expanding war.

What troubled Tojo Hideki, the former war minister who assumed the Japanese premiership in October 1941, was the realization that Japan, now under intense economic pressure, could achieve no compromise. To avoid both costly concessions

[51] Japanese note of May 12, 1941, *Foreign Relations, Japan*, II, 332–333.

[52] Herbert Feis, *The Road to Pearl Harbor*, pp. 215–216, 238.

and immediate hostilities, Tojo embarked on a dual policy of continuing diplomatic efforts even while completing operational preparations for a possible war.[53] To conduct his final negotiations with Hull, Tojo dispatched Kurusu Saburo, an experienced Japanese diplomat, to Washington. The Imperial Conference of November 5 gave Kurusu until November 25 to achieve an agreement. Thereafter the question of war would go before the emperor.

In Washington, Kurusu faced the challenge of ridding Japan of its enervating war in China, at least in part on Japanese terms, as well as a renewal of U.S.-Japanese trade. For these concessions he could offer an eventual Japanese withdrawal from all Indochina. On November 20, Kurusu presented this formula to Hull in a final proposal. Hull countered momentarily with a *modus vivendi* that differed but slightly from the Japanese offer. But Hull had also prepared a ten-point peace proposal that demanded a total Japanese withdrawal from China and Indochina in exchange for a new trade agreement. With much of the Chinese treaty structure at stake, Hull presented his *modus vivendi* to the British, Chinese, Australian, and Dutch ambassadors in Washington before making it a formal offer to Kurusu.[54] In this final crisis, Chiang Kai-shek managed to eliminate the *modus vivendi*. The American press, denouncing compromise as an invitation to war, joined Chinese officials in creating an intellectual and emotional barrier to compromise that the Roosevelt administration refused to challenge. For Roosevelt, war seemed to present fewer problems than reversing a decade of U.S. intentions in the Far East. On November 26, Hull pre-

[53] See Chihiro Hosoya, "Japan's Decision for War in 1941," *Hitotsubashi Journal of Law and Politics* 5 (April 1967): 12–14.

[54] Memorandum of conversations among Hull, Halifax, Hu Shih, Casey, and Loudon, November 24, 1941, between Hull and Halifax, November 25, 1941, between Hull and Hu Shih, November 25, 1941, PSF: Diplomatic Correspondence, Japan, Box 13, FDRL.

sented to Kurusu the ten-point program to bring the year's conversations to an end. For Kurusu, China's apparent control of U.S. policy was beyond comprehension.[55]

On December 1 the Imperial Conference in Tokyo made its fateful decision for war. Still, even as the Japanese task force moved toward Pearl Harbor, much of the Japanese high command scarcely anticipated a Japanese victory. Facing the choice between total capitulation and an unending war in China, Tokyo chose the most drastic response available—a direct attack on the U.S. Pacific fleet. Behind that decision lay a desire to fight under the most favorable conditions, to gain whatever advantage might accrue from the destruction of the U.S. fleet, and to reap the special dispensation of good fortune that a display of courage might bring. It was an act of desperation. As Tojo later phrased it, "sometimes a man has to jump with his eyes closed, from the temple of Kiyomizu into the ravine below."[56]

U.S. officials had miscalculated badly the effect of their inflexibility on Japanese decision making. Throughout the year of burgeoning crisis in the Far East, Roosevelt's advisers had based their optimism on two factors. First, they believed Japan so vulnerable to U.S. economic power that sanctions would compel its government to stop its assault on the Far Eastern treaty structure. Japan, indeed, was vulnerable, but no Japanese government, for both psychological and political reasons, would submit to moral and economic sanctions. By narrowing Japan's alternatives and introducing the factor of time, the economic pressure merely accelerated Japan's expansion and stiffened the decision for war.[57]

Second, members of the press and the administration as-

[55] For Hull's ten-point program and the Japanese reaction see *Peace and War*, pp. 807–810, 811–812.

[56] See Hosoya, "Japan's Decision for War," pp. 14–19; Hosoya, "Miscalculations in Deterrent Policy," p. 112.

[57] Stimson informed a cabinet meeting in October 1940 that "in the

sured Roosevelt repeatedly that Japan would, at any cost,
avoid war with the United States. In urging Roosevelt to avoid
a top-level conference with Premier Konoe in August 1941,
Hornbeck argued effectively that any settlement acceptable to
Japan would infringe on American principles. Beyond that, the
search for an agreement was not an urgent matter. "We are not
in great danger vis-à-vis Japan," he advised the president, "and
Japan . . . does not possess military capacity sufficient to warrant
an attack by her upon the United States."[58] Early in November
a recently returned young Foreign Service officer informed Hornbeck that the embassy staff in Tokyo feared that Japan, from
sheer desperation, would launch an attack on the United States.
"Tell me," replied Hornbeck, "of one case in history where a
nation went to war out of desperation."[59] As late as November
27, 1941, Hornbeck advised the administration that Japan, even
while launching possible new offensives in the Far East, would
endeavor to avoid war with the United States.[60] Armed with
such assurances of American invulnerability, Roosevelt never
recognized any need to pursue less than the unraveling of the
whole Japanese empire. He embarked cautiously but unerringly
toward a policy of escalation anchored to economic sanctions and
a limited show of force. With each major increment of pressure,
the country's dominant foreign policy elite anticipated a Japanese capitulation. But the capitulation never came.

autumn of 1919 President Wilson got his dander up and put on an
embargo on all cotton going to Japan and a boycott on her silk, with the
result that she crawled down within two months and brought all of her
troops out from Siberia like whipped puppies" (quoted in Hosoya, "Miscalculations in Deterrent Policy," p. 111).

[58] Hornbeck's argument of September 5, 1941, *Foreign Relations, 1941*,
IV, 425–426. See also Hornbeck's memorandum of August 30, 1941,
ibid., p. 412.

[59] James C. Thomson, Jr., "The Role of the Department of State," in
Pearl Harbor as History: Japanese-American Relations, 1931–1941, ed.
Dorothy Borg and Shumpei Okamoto, p. 101.

[60] *Foreign Relations, 1941*, IV, 673.

BIBLIOGRAPHY

Blakeslee, George H. "The Japanese Monroe Doctrine." *Foreign Affairs* 11 (July 1933): 671–678.

Borg, Dorothy. *The United States and the Far Eastern Crisis of 1933–1938*. Cambridge, Mass.: Harvard University Press, 1964.

Cohen, Warren I. "From Contempt to Containment: Cycles in American Attitudes toward China." In *Twentieth-Century American Foreign Policy*, edited by John Braeman, Robert H. Bremner, and David Brody. Columbus: Ohio State University Press, 1971.

Current, Richard N. "The Stimson Doctrine and the Hoover Doctrine." *American Historical Review* 59 (April 1954): 513–542.

Feis, Herbert. *The Road to Pearl Harbor*. New York: Atheneum, 1962.

Grew, Joseph C. *Turbulent Era: A Diplomatic Record of Forty Years, 1904–1945*. Edited by Walter Johnson. Boston: Houghton Mifflin, 1952.

Hosoya, Chihiro. "Japan's Decision for War in 1941." *Hitotsubashi Journal of Law and Politics* 5 (April 1967): 10–19.

———. "Miscalculations in Deterrent Policy: Japanese-U.S. Relations, 1938–1941." *Journal of Peace Research* (Oslo), no. 2 (1968), pp. 97–115.

Hull, Cordell. *Memoirs*. New York: Macmillan, 1948.

Ishii, Viscount Kikujiro. "The Permanent Bases of Japanese Foreign Policy." *Foreign Affairs* 11 (January 1933): 220–229.

Johnstone, William Crane. *The United States and Japan's New Order*. New York: Oxford University Press, 1941.

Moley, Raymond. *After Seven Years*. New York: Harper & Brothers, 1939.

Myers, William Starr. *The Foreign Policies of Herbert Hoover, 1929–1933*. New York: Charles Scribner's Sons, 1940.

President's Personal Files. Franklin D. Roosevelt Library, Hyde Park, New York.

President's Secretary's File. China, 1933–1936. Franklin D. Roosevelt Library, Hyde Park, New York.

———. Diplomatic Correspondence, Japan. Franklin D. Roosevelt Library, Hyde Park, New York.

————. Frank Knox. Franklin D. Roosevelt Library, Hyde Park, New York.

Roosevelt, Franklin D. *Franklin D. Roosevelt and Foreign Affairs.* Edited by Edgar B. Nixon. 3 vols. Cambridge, Mass.: Belknap Press of Harvard University Press, 1969.

Sternsher, Bernard. "The Stimson Doctrine: F.D.R. *versus* Moley and Tugwell." *Pacific Historical Review* 31 (August 1962): 281–289.

Stimson, Henry L. "Bases of American Foreign Policy during the Past Four Years." *Foreign Affairs* 11 (April 1933): 383–396.

————. *The Far Eastern Crisis: Recollections and Observations.* New York: Harper & Brothers, 1939.

————, and McGeorge Bundy. *On Active Service in Peace and War.* New York: Harper & Brothers, 1948.

Stromberg, Roland N. *Collective Security and American Foreign Policy.* New York: Praeger, 1963.

"Telling Tokyo Where We Stand." *Literary Digest*, January 23, 1932, pp. 5–6.

Thomson, James C., Jr. "The Role of the Department of State." In *Pearl Harbor as History: Japanese-American Relations, 1931–1941*, edited by Dorothy Borg and Shumpei Okamoto. New York: Columbia University Press, 1973.

United States Department of State. *Papers Relating to the Foreign Relations of the United States. Japan, 1931–1941.* 2 vols. State Department Publication no. 2008. Washington, D.C.: G.P.O., 1943.

————. *Papers Relating to the Foreign Relations of the United States, 1937.* 5 vols. State Department Publication no. 5435. Washington, D.C.: G.P.O., 1954.

————. *Papers Relating to the Foreign Relations of the United States, 1938.* 5 vols. State Department Publication no. 5775. Washington, D.C.: G.P.O., 1955.

————. *Peace and War: United States Foreign Policy, 1931–1941.* State Department Publication no. 1983. Washington, D.C.: G.P.O., 1943.

"Why Stimson's Speech Stirs Up Japan." *Literary Digest*, August 20, 1932, p. 6.

Wilbur, Ray Lyman, and Arthur Mastick Hyde, eds. *The Hoover Policies.* New York: Charles Scribner's Sons, 1937.